QUANTUM SOUND
MIRACLE
iQUBE™

7 QUANTUM HACKS
TO TRANSFORM YOUR
HEALING BUSINESS

HELENA REILLY, MA

Reilly, Helena.
Quantum Sound Miracle iQube: 7 Quantum Hacks To Transform Your Healing Business. 1st Edition.

Editing by Nina Shoroplova | NinaShoroplova.ca
Book Formatting by AmitDey | amitdey2528@gmail.com

ISBN: 978-1-64669-587-4

1. Change (Psychology) 2. Thought and Thinking. 3. New Thought.

Advance Praise

I find Quantum Sound Miracle iQube *to be an enlightening read. It is indisputable that we live in a sea of energy and that energy has a huge effect on the quality of our lives. The book provides a great summary of energy concepts and is a good first step in investigating the use of sound to improve energy alignment."*

Sidney Bostian,
Clinical Professor, Finance Insurance &
Real Estate at Virginia Commonwealth University

This book Quantum Sound Miracle iQube *is a goldmine of information and inspiration. What really struck me was the part about that we constantly design all the external things in our lives from our homes to our diets, everything we can see, but we rarely think about what we can't see. It's what we can't see that really needs to be addressed! Thank God for the Miracle iQube and the Voice Code Software.*

Reading this book really clarified many things for me and has me so excited to embark upon my Quantum Sound Healing mission!

Having this technology in my life is truly a Divine intervention!

Shannon McGough,
Marketing Consultant,
Certified Yoga Instructor, Professional Dancer

It is a book that opens a new journey road for your life and your loved ones too.

George Eleftheriadis,
Professional Builder, Engineer, and Designer

If you are looking for a shortcut to lasting transformation, this book is the guide to getting better results from your personal development efforts, and for your clients in your healing practice.

The Miracle IQube and Voice Activated Sound Therapy have helped me to discover and follow my path in life with greater sense of conviction, grace, and ease.

I found that the book describes quite lucidly "how the Miracle technology works" to penetrate the subconscious, allowing me to rescript my life on a vibrational level.

Whatever modality you are implementing in your healing practice and everyday life, this is the missing modality that, once implemented, will transform the results in your business and life.

Even though I am very active in personal development, prior to working with this technology, I experienced dissatisfaction in many areas of my life, including relationships, money, and emotional well-being. It was like I was constantly fighting an upward battle that seems to make progress very slowly.

After I started to listen to the voice analysis tapes daily while sleeping with the Miracle IQube next to my bed, I experienced a profound level of breakthroughs. I used to believe that I needed love and affection from a romantic partner, a few million dollars, and a flat stomach to feel and be whole and worthy. This has now shifted to a deep knowingness in the gut that I already am whole and worthy and I feel that. With this shift, I now experience a sense of lasting peace and freedom. Ironically, I also sense the things I wanted are coming to me more now because I'm not resisting them by persisting with the "not having it yet" story.

I highly recommend this technology and this book to anyone who is on the personal- and spiritual-development journey. After attending dozens of Tony Robbins's seminars, silent meditations, breathwork sessions, and energy healing retreats, I can attest that this tool will 10x or more your development on every level! God bless you.

Jimmy Wang,
Financial Consultant, Entrepreneur
and Day Trader

The Quantum Sound Miracle iQube *is a game changer!*

This book describes the anti-anxiety, well-being medicine of the future delivered in 7 Quantum Hacks.

Helena's quantum hacks clarify how the technology works to penetrate beyond the stories my clients present with, into the depth of the subconscious where everything is being scripted. They also gave me the insight into how to use this breakthrough technology at a deeper level to improve client results in my healing business, as well as harmonizing my own state of well-being as a healer. This balance is a necessity in today's anxious, high-paced world.

The book grounds the esoteric quantum knowledge into a practical, easy-to-understand and follow process. It's a paint-by-numbers approach to quantum transformation.

I have been using the Quantum Sound iQube in my healing practice for six years and it has been extremely effective in assisting clients with grounding, leading to shifts in their consciousness. This greatly enhances each client's ability to alter their perspective.

Overall I have found it to be the most valuable and effective tool I've encountered in shifting consciousness in my twenty-three years of practice.

If you are seeking to optimize the results in your healing business and life, this book will reveal seven secret shortcuts that will enhance your well-being while improving your clients' results.

The book speaks to the essential need of healers and coaches to create their own sanctuary to discharge, recharge, and align.

Kerri Finnecy,
H.H.P. Energy Healing Business Owner

This groundbreaking book gave me the insight that I needed to understand the profound shifts that have occurred in my life over the last year since the Miracle iQube entered my life.

It helped to clarify the impactful seven quantum shortcuts that have transformed my relationships and my business. When I combined the 7 Quantum Hacks into one potent technology, my life transformed like magic. It is like engaging seven powerful armies to work behind the scenes, enabling lifelong patterns of depression and anxiety to loosen their hold on my daily life and relationships.

It is as though I made quantum leaps without truly understanding all of the dynamics at play.

It is with great appreciation that I write this letter saying "THANK YOU" to Bob and Helena for bringing this wonderful technology to the world. The Miracle iQube and Quantum Sound Therapy with Voice Code Analysis is a powerful modality. They comprise the 7 Quantum Hacks that can bring about instant relief from the environment and stresses of everyday life. Since I have been using this technology, I have found comfort and stress-free living with new confidence to overcome any obstacles on my path! I highly recommend this for every healing business owner, home, and school to help implement the tools we all need to succeed at all our endeavors.

Thank you, with ALL my heart

Donna McCondichie,
Realtor, Alternative Healing Business Owner

Dedication

For Robert Lloy, my co-creator and soul mate, the mystic and genius who envisioned, nurtured, and developed this work as part of a more evolved future for humanity. My only true wish is that this work turns into something greater than us—a movement that effortlessly transforms you, your world, your business, and humanity.

Acknowledgements

I would like to thank Geoff Affleck of GeoffAffleck.com for stepping in to provide his extensive resources to shape this book into its final form. Deep felt thanks to Nina Shoroplova of NinaShoroplova.ca who treated this as a labor of love instead of just another business contract. Thank you, Nina, for despite my obvious flaws as a writer, you intuitively understood that this is a work to help humanity understand the 7 Quantum Hacks. In many ways, Nina acted as the midwife to this book, by nurturing it until it could stand on its own. Thank you for the input of the editors Zoe MacFarland and Rebecca Coates who helped clarify the message.

I thank Marci Shimoff of happyfornoreason.com for agreeing to write the Foreword and generously offering to help support and expand this mission in the world. I thank Robert Lloy my partner for ingeniously "imagining and creating his vision of an awakened humanity" and for meticulously inventing the healing tools for tomorrow. I thank Ian Burton who oversees the physical creation of this work and perfects the Quantum Sound iQubes so that they take a viable future form in the world of tomorrow.

Contents

Foreword

by
Marci Shimoff

*E*nergetically speaking, it's a crazy world out there these days. The sheer amount of static or noise from various electromagnetic fields that bombard us every day is massive. The onslaught may be invisible but the effects are palpable—anxiety, fatigue, depression, to name just a few. It all throws us off balance, and we're left struggling to find our center, no matter how disciplined we are in our daily practices.

As this energetic interference continues to grow, it's becoming clearer that we need a quantum shift in the energetic support available to us. Helena Reilly has dedicated over twenty-five years of her life to offer this specific support to humanity at this time.

I first met Helena when she joined my yearlong mentoring program, Your Year of Miracles, in which I help thousands of women around the world live in the flow by creating the conditions where miracles can occur. I soon learned just how closely aligned our work was when she told me her mission and introduced me to the Quantum Miracle iQube.

As an author and transformational teacher focusing on happiness and success for the last twenty-five years myself,

I've been exposed to and researched countless transformational modalities. I'm so impressed by and grateful for the "quantum work" Helena Reilly is doing. It's the real deal.

I'm not a scientist so I don't understand exactly *how* the Quantum Miracle iQube works but I understand the idea of *why* it works. More importantly, I've experienced it powerfully working in my own life.

When I first received my iQube and set it up in the office, I immediately noticed a subtle yet very tangible shift in the quality of the energy. It felt as if the energy around me became cleaner and there was more fluidity in the space. Within the first few days, I could even recognize when it wasn't on. After the first month of having the iQube, I was feeling better in my body and experiencing greater clarity in my mind. I also noticed that some old obstacles came up for healing, but they quickly dissipated as though they were being released into a "quantum vortex." It felt as though I was flowing more easily *with* the river rather than *against* it.

Many amazing things have happened since I've started using the Miracle iQube, and while I could be saying, "*Wow, this is coincidental,*" I don't think it is. New opportunities for my business have come to me, and people have offered support in ways they hadn't happened before. Based on what I've experienced, I believe that this technology supports a state of effortless flow—what I call "The Miracle Zone"—where wonderful synchronicities become common occurrences.

With the Miracle iQube, we have a greater ability to rewrite the script and alter the trajectory of our life. How wonderful that it plays 24-7 providing support while we sleep, eat, play, and work.

This technology is a gift for humanity and a game changer as living in energetic coherence becomes more a necessity than a luxury. This may be particularly helpful for people who work in the fields of healing, coaching, and transformation, where it's imperative to stay in their highest energy while helping others.

Hallelujah! It's about time for technology like this to support us in living our best lives. Thank you so much, Helena, for bringing this forward for our evolution, our happiness, and the peace of our planet.

Marci Shimoff, #1 NY Times best-selling author *Happy for No Reason, Love for No Reason,* and *Chicken Soup for the Woman's Soul*

PART I

CHAPTER 1

The Quantum Game Changer

Adding the Missing Modality to Skyrocket Your Client Results

*A*re you looking to add a modality to your energy healing business? One that cracks the subconscious code so you can stay energized *and* provide your clients with the solution to their challenges?

I know that you have been searching for this missing piece. This breakthrough modality I am so excited about could be the magic recipe for you, as the owner of a healing or coaching business, to thrive personally and in turn get better results in your healing business and your life. You've been searching for that elusive ingredient that allows you to raise the frequency and results for your clients and your practice. To find that new octave of possibility that shifts you from strive to thrive. The missing jigsaw piece that will raise your frequency and that of your clients to a new octave of possibilities.

If you are seeking to speed up the results in your healing business, tap into your intuition and manifest the highest best results for your life and your clients' lives, then you are in the right place at the right time.

You are ready for the next step. That is why you have found this book at this time. There is absolutely no accident in the synchronicity of this.

This book found you.

You have likely been searching for something that will get your healer mojo back quickly without investing thousands of hours in a new program or modality. Think of this book as being as significant to you as oxygen is to your body—only way more fun and experiential.

What I am about to share in the chapters ahead will give you an unfair advantage. It provides a quantum leap whereby you will find yourself more fulfilled and more productive, without investing thousands of hours in the learning and application of thousands of tiny details about the body, physiology, the psyche, and the emotions. Thanks to my decades in this industry, you get to skip the sweat and go straight to the soiree.

These 7 Quantum Hacks will open you up to co-create with your higher, intuitive self—your spirit—effortlessly. Their purpose is to give you shortcuts to master the energy of your work. The great thing, too, is that it doesn't matter what line of energy, coaching, or self-help service you deliver; this system will cut through all the garbage and get you straight to the gold.

I use the word *quantum* because these hacks work at multiple levels of existence and multiple dimensions of consciousness, often beyond your current awareness. (I explain more about *quantum* in chapter 3).

You won't need to travel to an exotic location, take hallucinogens, or learn the entire anatomy of the physical body, the energy field, or the emotions to benefit.

It is for these reasons that I have called this book *Quantum Sound Miracle iQube: 7 Quantum Hacks to Get Better Results in Your Healing Business*. We are now living in the information age, so it is necessary to find the shortcuts that deliver the ineffable well-being that has become so elusive.

If you're ready to integrate new advantages to get you ahead of the game, then I'm ready to share the secrets it has taken me over thirty-five years to uncover. Together, my partner Robert Lloy and I have been researching and developing this area of consciousness for over eighty years. When I refer to *we* and *our* in this book, I am referring to Robert and myself.

Together, these seven hacks create our Quantum Sound Therapy modality. Several are bundled within our Quantum Sound Miracle iQube, the centerpiece of an incredible system that shifts your frequency 24-7 through Scalar Wave technology and sound frequencies so you can live your life empowered. This creates an enormous field of quantum energy. In fact, it creates sound waves that simultaneously clear and cleanse the environment while raising the resonance of everyone within the field. More details to come.

This missing modality that employs quantum healing will increase the effectiveness of your work and help you stand out from the masses by dazzling your clients and speeding up the results you deliver for them. All without the grind you see your peers undergoing to produce lackluster results. Consider my results the faster, better, stronger hack for any healing or coaching professional, the "10×" you've been waiting for to amplify your practice without extra effort.

You may be thinking, "But I'm not a healer-coach!"

It is my observation that you are. Whatever the delivery of your healing modality, you are on a path of transformation for your clients. Healers are the new coaches; coaches are the new healers. Whether you identify with one or the other, know that the results are the same for your practice: magnified results, happier clients, and better profits.

I know you are wondering if there is a secret hack—a magical ingredient that you could add to your business or life that would make your clients and business thrive on all levels. And, of course, something that would make you feel exhilarated again—in the zone—more uplifted and lighter at the end of your day, every day of your life. Something that would help you to truly stand out in your work and purpose.

Once this ingredient is added, your dreams can turn toward tapping into your intuition more easily and speeding up positive results for your clients. Great results create the raving fans and the referrals you are seeking! With great results come great word-of-mouth opportunities, and your business thrives. Like the domino effect, you in turn feel happier, more balanced, and content because you're effecting change in your community. This enhances your connection to your intuitive self so you can effortlessly co-create with spirit to serve. It all leads to optimal results in your healing practice.

I make it sound so easy, right?

It *is* easy when you have the answers.

Consider this the quantum shortcut for accelerating your results while you optimize your state of well-being. How would it feel to rapidly convert your clients to raving fans, so more referrals and bookings pour in?

Feeling fulfilled, inspired, and awakened again would open new doors of possibility that help you expand and take off in new and unexpected ways. This infectious feeling of well-being will spread to others, and this alone will open new doors and opportunities for you to expand.

While there is excitement about not just meeting but transcending your healer-coach goals, there is likely a little voice telling you that you can't do it alone. You're already aware of the challenges of operating your own business. You've experienced the number of hats you have to wear to deliver across all aspects of your practice, and you're unsure if you can add in more steps, even if they are attractive shortcuts! You feel the need for greater support to truly fulfill your mission and purpose as a healer. At the end of the day, you might at times feel that you have picked up energies from your clients that are not your own but they stick to you like glue.

You do not have to do it alone.

The Secret Sauce

Three nights before Christmas Eve 2018, at 8:45 p.m., I received an unexpected phone call from Tony Robbins's personal assistant. She was calling to purchase the Quantum Sound Miracle for Tony and his wife Sage. I learned later that Sage Robbins intuitively felt, and was searching for, something greater, something "straight outta quantum" that they could add to their daily routine, the secret sauce that would keep the vibes as high as possible.

You can imagine my surprise. This was for the family of one of the most successful transformational leaders in the world! Even *they* were searching for the hacks to make quantum changes effortlessly and bypass the toil and hard work on the path to unleashing their power.

Sage knew intuitively that there was something she could add to their lives that would raise the vibration and increase harmony, well-being, and quality of life for both their family and their tribe of co-creators.

What she didn't know at the time was that it could hum quietly in the corner without requiring constant attention. A well-being technology. As consciousness leaders, the Robbinses are committed to keeping the vibrational altitude in their home at its peak. Like a seeker searching in the Himalayas for the master hidden in the cave, she was searching for the secret sauce that would allow the highest vibrations to be maintained as effortlessly as possible. This is what they call "in state."

Several weeks later, I was invited as a guest to attend Tony's Business Mastery Seminar in West Palm Beach. I had the good fortune to meet one of the coaches in the elevator on our way to breakfast. The coach explained how much effort he put into going into an optimal state before working with a coaching client on the phone. That coach's efforts included willfully getting himself "in state" by breathing, exercising, meditating, and doing yoga. This was before he found our Quantum Healing Sound system.

The Life Lesson

Here's my life lesson. Even world-class coaches and healers require consistent support, and are in search of tools that will harmonize their lives. They are seeking the flow state, or perhaps a unique energy signature that will uplift their resonance even while they sleep, eat, work, and meditate. They are also very aware that while they are working within a group context, they are the influencers of the energetic state of the group. As such, it is a pivotal issue for them to maintain the highest frequency possible in order to optimize their positive influence.

Sound familiar?

I know you put your heart and soul into your healing business. You are amazing at what you do. It is truly your gift for humanity. You likely have more than one certificate hanging on your wall to show the world what you have learned through countless hours of dedicated work. You truly have a desire to help people and serve the planet. *Many of you intend to expand your mission so you can help thousands, or even millions, of people during your lifetime. Herein lies the problem. How much of you is there to go around? If you get out of balance or drained, how will your day-to-day feel?*

Despite your feeling that it is your mission to help thousands of people transform and thrive, your daily reality has its challenges. Perhaps it's an issue of time—or lack thereof—to take care of your own needs and to rebalance, particularly after seeing clients who can be energetically draining. You want to meditate or do yoga, you would love to spend time in nature, and it may even seem out of reach to make time to stop and smell the roses, to breathe and chill.

If I'm Such a Great Healer ...?

We have all heard about burnout. And even wondered, "Burnout! If I'm such a great healer, why do I feel like crap?" Perhaps you feel you have picked up some energy entanglements from clients. How do you release these? Where do you find the time? How do you protect yourself from the energy projections and releases of others?

I can tell you from experience that this lack of self-care time is kryptonite for the healer-coach. If you invest too much time in the giving zone and don't find the time for yourself, burnout is inevitable. It's imperative to find a zone where you can discharge the energy and emotions that your antennae pick up during the day.

"But I'm so busy!"

When this is your visceral response, it's time to address the problems with time.

Let's dig a little deeper here.

Ask Yourself

Ask yourself these questions to see if the quantum shortcuts will help you save time and energy and protect your well-being for decades to come. My mission is for you to learn to shine and share your light to its fullest potential. *If you honestly answer yes to one of these questions, I may have a soul-ution that will work for you.*

Which of these is a "Hell, yes!" for you?

- ✓ Do you wish you could add a modality to your business that would help you get better results for your clients while supporting your intuition, inspiration, and brilliance?
- ✓ When you look in the mirror, do you see the energy and stress of your last client(s)?
- ✓ Has your healing business become more of a burden than a joy? Do you feel you've lost the mojo that galvanized your decision to step up as a healer?

✓ Do you feel that you promise more than you deliver? Are your results too vague or slow to materialize for your clients to become raving fans?

✓ Do you feel that if you fail to master the energy of your business, it will have a negative impact on your personal and intimate relationships?

✓ Do you feel that your healing business is lacking an essential ingredient that will synchronize and shift your results? Even with mastery and passion for your modality, is there still something missing that could sink you into oblivion?

✓ Are you missing the support that will lift your clients (and yourself) and keep positive results and referrals flowing?

✓ Do you have a sense of burden and fear around attracting more clients (and therefore inviting burnout), even though it would provide ongoing financial success?

✓ Do you feel that your clients are increasingly stressed, distressed, and anxious?

✓ Are you concerned about where to find your sanctuary, serenity, "me time," peace, and pleasure?

✓ Are the relaxation techniques you've tried not cutting it?

✓ Have you lost the peace you thought you would have when you created and designed your ideal life as a healer?

✓ Where and how are you rewarding yourself?

Do you want the good news or the good news?

If you're looking for a shortcut to shift from being a struggling, overwhelmed practitioner to operating a thriving, profitable business, my 7 Quantum Hacks condense a lifetime of work into a simple formula. This book is a shortcut for you. In each of the 7 Quantum Hacks, I have condensed one simple formula that took years for us to create.

You can use each hack for the rest of your life. Each hack combines every element of the energy field surrounding and supporting your life—your mind, body, soul, and field.

This secret miracle ingredient involves you and your clients vibrating at higher levels. You're going to learn about rewiring and "upwiring" the brain (see more about the term *upwiring* in chapter 3: "Hack 1") and about how to release deep, pent-up, subconscious energy blocks that have halted your and your clients' progress so far—no matter the modality you've employed. My secrets are the complementary tools to run alongside your primary healing practice, to support and solidify your life's work. They are simple, precise, and effortless.

My mission is designed to support your mission: to willfully move into the state of consciousness that allows you to connect to your infinite potential and the dynamic field of possibility. To use your brain as an antenna that picks up the sound waves, light waves, and scalar energy that you require—that you need—to fulfill your mission.

Are you ready to hear how my own journey inspired this solution?

In the next chapter, I will share a small part of the journey that led me to co-create the 7 Quantum Hacks so that you can have a smoother ride while you fulfill your purpose as a healer.

Have a question for me? Feel free to sign up for a "Find Your Frequency" consult with me at calendly.com/quantum-soundtherapy. I will tell you which notes are stressed and which ones are weak in your Voice Code.

See what others have asked and ask your own questions at quantumsoundtherapy.com/contact-us. I want to hear from you.

CHAPTER 2

Incognito

It Is Safer to Hide

D o you ever wonder how an author reaches this point? Why and how I came to write this book for you? Where and when the desire to communicate the huge possibilities overrode my fear of being vulnerable about writing my life story?

I wrote this book because I have been where you are, searching for the missing ingredient that would transform my life and my clients' lives. Some modality that they couldn't resist or deny the efficacy of. A modality that was results-oriented and that would transform the subconscious without so much struggle. Getting them off the emotional roller-coaster ride of the primitive, reptilian brain that was controlling their lives is indeed my priority to this very day.

Also, a modality that would offer them a transformation that wasn't just a fleeting experiential high, like so many are seeking today. Instead, a modality that they could integrate into their own lives and their own fields of energy, before burnout sets in or inspiration is lost.

Are you simply seeking to crack the healing code and get the results that your healing clients deserve?

A part of my purpose is to inspire you on your mission. The heart of my mission is to attract and activate a wider circle to awaken effortlessly, while supporting the efforts of the healers and coaches who are dedicated to making a phenomenal difference in people's lives.

<<<|>>>

I want to stop right here and have you breathe deeply into your belly. It is okay for you to shine, to prosper, and to be brilliant at your work. My intent is that you will somehow, magically, through synchronism, find this book, and that it will act as a reminder from your soul.

<<<|>>>

I have a deep knowing that I was put on this earth to write this book for you, and I have been waiting for the time to be right, so that it ends up in the hands of you, an awakened healer.

This book is a culmination of my life experience of journeying as a healer.

I did not have a near-death experience in which I saw God and she told me to be a healer, and overnight I was instantly enlightened and started writing books.

I am not your guru. I am not writing this book with the ease of a best-selling maven. Instead, I have chipped away at my inner mission my entire life. In fact, it goes against the grain for me, because I would prefer to hide.

An Intuitive Since Birth

I've always been intuitive. I have been in the healing business my entire life. I was born with the gifts of claircognizance, clairsentience, and clairaudience, giving me the ability to feel the problem someone is experiencing. I was able to feel and know their karmic blocks—their obstacles—and address them in simple words. As a child, I could perceive that adults found this quite unsettling, so I learned to keep my mouth shut and hide this gift. This pattern of hiding hurt me deeply. Withholding a precious gift blocks your energy, your flow. I didn't know how to handle or express what I was intuitively seeing and knowing in words that didn't hurt or scare people. For adults, my gift was alarming; yet, I was considered a good influence on other kids and "rented out" as such. If the other kids got aggressive as a result, I would withdraw.

Even today, I still don't have the right words to console the pain I witness. Whether it's fear, loss, anxiety, or depression, it reveals itself to me like a bug under a microscope. I can see when people have been traumatized or abused and also when they are about to commit violent acts. Illness appears to me like blocked energy; there's a certain look in the eyes. It might sound weird, but it's like I walk around with more information about someone than the person themself has. I can tell if someone is into kinky or abusive behavior.

The beginning of my journey into explorations of consciousness using alternative awakening modalities began in my childhood, even before I was aware that this was my mission in life.

I have paid attention to the odd synchronicities that have consistently appeared in my life. With this attunement to opportunity, I have walked through the doorways presented to me to discover what was ready to be revealed. I've seized those moments to implement and create what I intuitively knew needed to be birthed into the world. There was no script for what was about to be created. Those moments of awakening include discovering that Timothy Leary's first communal Harvard University LSD experiment occurred a convenient two blocks from my house in Newton, Massachusetts.

And when I read about the immortal Herakhan Babaji in the *Yoga Journal* and found myself, after a number of synchronicities, walking next to him several months later on a fifteen-kilometer trek to his ashram in the Himalayas. I was taught directly by him for several months and was able to have conversations and ask him questions daily. After meditating in his presence for a couple of months and asking him questions freely, my deeper questions about the human soul, emotions, and psyche were answered.

I also spontaneously see certain parts of a person's past and future, and I know at the same time whether I am able to intervene and alter this beneficially. This has also been a little unsettling for the people around me. For example, when I co-owned a financial firm, there was an investment in rare coins that I thought was rather dubious. I had no evidence to substantiate this, though. I went to sleep one night and awoke with four words in my mind: THE COINS ARE JUNK. That was it. Although I shared the warning, no one listened. Eight years later, the scam was revealed.

My First Psychic Reading, Age Three

As a three-year-old, I had a vision. I made the mistake of wandering downstairs from my bedroom perch and sharing this openly with my parents. This began my lifelong pattern of hiding or obscuring what I knew and saw. This experience also initiated the pattern of self-doubt, insecurity, and self-denial that almost destroyed me. I share this because I believe that many of you have also shut down automatically and repressed the genius gift that you are here to share.

At the time, we were living in affluence in a nine-bedroom, nine-bathroom home in Newton, Massachusetts. My parents' bedroom was larger than most two-bedroom condos, and we even had maid's quarters, though no maid. It was isolating for a toddler and I felt very lonely.

When the vision came, I naturally described it to my parents in detail, not having yet mastered the need to filter what I saw. I channeled the future for them. Now some would call this a "future-self jump."

I remember going downstairs in my yellow footed pajamas. I was very excited, as I had just seen something I urgently wanted to share. So I simply said: "You are rich now, but someday you will be poor and many people will live in the rooms of your house." When I saw the look of shock on my mother's face, I knew instantly that I had seen precisely what she feared. Her future was not as she would have hoped. I also knew that she realized I had the family "gift" of healing and sight that my maternal grandmother possessed. It was at that precise moment I learned I had to hide what I saw, knew, felt, and heard if I wanted to please my parents. I became invisible. I realized that who I was and what I saw were something to be feared, shied away from, and hidden. It was at this moment that I shut down my abilities and decided that in order to survive, I had to cover my truth. Unfortunately, my prophecy came true thirty years later.

So of course, in my own confusion, and in my desire to better understand these flashes of insight into people and the future, I became a therapist.

The Deep Dive into Karmic Patterns

When I work with someone I can see whatever might play out in their lives, relating to an issue or a block, and what may have occurred in the past that's stored as a memory in the subconscious. With my clients, in my private practice on Manhattan's Upper West Side, it would appear as a picture memory that was the root cause of their presenting issue or problem. Once I had visualized their memory experience, I would use past-life-regression hypnosis and Voice Code Analysis so that my client would revisit the memory and release it. I like to think of the Quantum Sound (Scalar Optimized Sound) as an optimized surround-sound that simultaneously harmonizes the client's energy field and chakras while raising the resonance of the environment. I use the analogy of having a continuous stream of energy healers present, doing their subtle magic.

In private practice, these gifts were very handy: I was being paid to help people see and resolve what was subconsciously blocking them from living the life of their dreams. As a result, I instantly had a waiting list of several months.

I had to do something with what I was seeing and knowing. At the age of fifteen, I started working in the Newton Mental Health Center as an intern therapist. This was the basis of my early curiosity about healing and therapeutic practices. The late Dr. Hal Cohen trained me as a psychoanalyst, because that's what he did at that clinic. This meant I had to do process-recording for every hour I spent with a client, which included writing down everything the client said and my responses to them. This habit has stuck with me, and I can review conversations as though they are on a screen. This is similar to the way I view the Akashic records.

This process of memorizing and recording conversations often proves annoying, as I'm readily able to pull up details of a conversation, no matter how long ago it occurred. I was always seeking the truth of what I could perceive would help people recover from their blockages, so I moved from psychotherapy to studying alternative healing modalities.

These days, you'd call me an empath or a highly sensitive person. Perhaps I am an old soul or an indigo child or a crystal child. But I grew up a while ago, and we didn't have those terms back then. There certainly wasn't the internet, to instantly figure out the meaning of what I was experiencing. I simply struggled with what appeared to be a weakness, and I hid from others what I saw and knew about them.

When I was all of eighteen, my father visited me at the restaurant where I was working as a waitress, the 99 Steak House. He said I could no longer work there, as he owned a corporation and he didn't want his friends seeing his daughter serving food. So instead I went to Harvard University, met Lawrence Kohlberg and some of his graduate students, studied with the clinicians, and got a cool internship.

My joke was that I went to the University of Chicago graduate school to learn what crazy was so that I wouldn't get myself in trouble by sharing some vision that no one around me understood. I learned to hide my gifts more, and to use conventional language.

As much as I could see the past, present, and future, I was also able to see, feel, and understand that the modalities being used—all of them, even the best—were all "blah, blah, blah." It was evident to me that the modalities were changing nothing. The block was being reinforced in the client's brain.

By the way, what I was seeing was confirmed when Gurumayi Chidvilasananda invited a group of therapists to the ashram in South Fallsburg, New York, for a special event. She had a NASA brain scientist show us EEG images of the brain that proved that when we hash out our problems by talking about them constantly, it reinforces or strengthens the trauma in the brain.

My intuition was correct!

Despite this awareness, I pursued my professional degree in individual, family, couples, and group therapy at the University of Chicago, where they gave me a full scholarship. This, however, seemed to be more blah, blah, blah.

It wasn't until I was working as a therapist and diagnostician at the ashram of Gurumayi Chidvilasananda in Ganeshpuri, India, that the light went on. I had been invited to use my apparent gift to answer questions for Gurumayi. When someone was having emotional, psychological, spiritual, or mental difficulties and they were referred to Gurumayi, she would refer them to me and my peer, Dr. Patrick Gillette, a British psychiatrist. Dr. Gillette did the initial interview, and it was my job to provide the diagnosis. The ashram gave me a typewriter. First, I went into an elaborate reading of the Akashic records. Then Gurumayi sent me a message: "Answer two questions: Was it this lifetime or another? Mother or father?" Then the treatment would proceed. Dr. Gillette would then decide whether he or I would do the treatment, which mostly consisted of talk therapy. However, we were experimenting with breath, energy healing, and a multiple of modalities to get results. We even had the ashram provide us with a teepee for energy and breathwork.

It was then that I saw that nothing—*nothing*—worked! As I was seeing a diverse range of yoga and meditation students who were visiting or living at the Ganeshpuri ashram, I slowly began to realize that the yoga, meditation, chanting, and *darshan* and *seva* practices did not penetrate a certain layer of the wounded subconscious. Even though at times the yoga practices would release these memories, there were many memories that remained hidden in dark recesses of the subconscious, manifesting in the relationships or life circumstances, or waiting to manifest.

This was my epiphany. I needed something—a psychic drill of sorts—that would reach these hidden memories and release them!

Even being in the presence of a fully realized master in an ashram in India practicing meditation, mantras, *seva* (selfless service), and self-inquiry—even sleeping in this ashram—did not reach the deep recesses of the subconscious mind. I realized that the subconscious mind was unwittingly scripting the world that we create and live in.

This proved both enlightening and devastating. It was the paradox. Nothing worked to reach the subtle realms of consciousness where we are co-creating our script.

When I was sent back into the world and told that my dharma was to somehow continue the work as a healer, I went with one intention: I would find or create a practice that dealt efficiently with the subconscious and transformed people's lives instantly. I had no idea what this intention would lead me to create.

This book is the culmination of the insights I discovered and created in the years after what I consider to be my "ashram experiment."

The Turning Point in My Story

I had been working with the late Don Campbell. Don was a renowned music visionary and teacher and the bestselling author of *The Mozart Effect*. During his lifetime, he contributed profoundly to the foundation of sound healing as we know it today. He convinced the world that music—specifically, the music of Mozart—could enhance learning. Of course we now understand that the reason music enhances learning is because of its inherent ability to entrain the brain into states, like alpha brainwave states, that are more conducive to learning.

Don had invited me to work with him in Boulder, Colorado, and the offer was still on the table when he sent me to the University of Honolulu to attend an event with a leading musicologist. To my surprise, the very first version of the technology created by Robert Lloy showed up! Rytwin Lee, a health and wellness practitioner, was demonstrating Robert's Voice Analysis technology and his unique sound-frequency formulas. Rytwin was one of the early adopters of one of Robert's first inventions—the Voice Analysis software delivery system. He was sharing Robert's work at this small gathering at the University. Rytwin played a series of frequencies from Robert's soundtrack. The one I remember was "Christ Consciousness," because I immediately went into samadhic trance. Information was conveyed to me instantly that this would be my life's work. I invited Rytwin to my home to conduct a Sound Laboratory. At the first session, I experienced a miracle.

Sound Laboratory: The First Miracle

We agreed to have Sound Laboratories at my home over-looking the Pacific Ocean, at Hawaii Loa Ridge, on Tuesdays at 7:30 p.m. I invited every alternative practitioner, acupuncturist, massage therapist, psychiatrist, energy healer, and so on to my home to experience this new Voice Analysis modality developed by Robert Lloy. We simply chose one person from the audience and did a voice analysis, and then delivered the soundtrack that had been generated by the software.

We were in for a big surprise when the very first participant called me the day after the very first Sound Laboratory to thank me and tell me that her doctor had cancelled her emergency surgery. When I asked her why, she explained that she was scheduled to have kidney stones removed. When she returned to her doctor the day after the event, the kidney stones had dissolved.

We continued the Sound Laboratories for several months at my home, until my family decided to move to New York.

The Genius Zen Zone

I will share the shortcuts that will allow you to remain in the Zen zone of genius, insight, and wellness.

Robert Lloy had been working tirelessly for many years creating a Voice Analysis software program. Within a couple of months, I purchased one technology system from him and opened a private practice in Manhattan. I knew the first day I met Robert that he was my joint mission partner, and we have been co-creating this work ever since.

During my practice years in Manhattan, I was also juggling the pressures of having a husband with a high-level corporate job and a nine-year-old son who played ice hockey. The hockey involved traveling by car hundreds of miles each week for practices, games, and tournaments. These pressures manifested in me as chronic fatigue syndrome (CFS). I sought out every alternative healing modality on the planet. CFS proved to be my lesson in the fall from grace of unlimited energy and potential.

When I learned that being in a field of healing sound, discharging draining energies, and consciously creating a supportive lifestyle would heal me, I realized I needed to change my lifestyle to one that supported my sensitivities and nurtured me. This enabled me to help others to heal.

My path has not been all insights and enlightenment. Yet, even while my path was not as instant as it will be for you when you implement what you read in this book, these are the steps I took to co-create a greater path to wellness and awakening, what I now call "raising my frequency." These steps—my 7 Quantum Hacks—will allow you to stay in your zone of well-being, avoiding the roadblocks and the long recovery I had to stumble through.

You don't need my abilities, just my insights.

CHAPTER 3

Upgrade Your Future Self

*I*n Part II of this book, I will share the 7 Quantum Hacks that will transform your practice automatically so that you can keep doing what you love and create a profitable business at the same time. As you tackle each chapter, I will unveil each hack you need to be even more brilliant in your work.

Consider these hacks like the upgrades for your smartphone, but instead of getting a couple a year, you're going to be continually advancing to the next operating system. These reboots work across your business, your relationships, your home, and yourself. With each one, life becomes easier.

I'm not bringing you a new way to meditate. Or a yoga pose you need to do daily. Or an instruction to get in ice water, drink only garlic juice for a week, or attach leeches to your skin. I'm not offering a woo-woo solution that offers vague and undefinable results. You'll find nothing in this book about smudging, doing headstands, or detoxing. This book explains a quantum-science-backed, mathematically derived technological modality to transcend the ho-hum hamster wheel that so many get trapped on, circling continually in search of answers to problems locked in the subconscious. Maybe this is the first time you've heard of using quantum physics to heal, but my partner Robert Lloy and I have spent our lifetimes working on unlocking quantum secrets to deliver quantum sound technology that works. With what I'm about to reveal, you may feel we've skipped into a futuristic sci-fi novel. But this is real.

Our well-integrated modality, developed over forty years, can lighten the burden of your load as a healer as you use it to get better results both in your practice (through the removal of subconscious blocks) and in your home, and even in your clients' homes. It is a modality that supports and enhances every other modality. It does not prescribe and treat—it supports and enhances.

When you employ 7 Quantum Hacks, you can expect to skyrocket your results, to keep you at the top of your game so you can co-create with spirit and help thousands of people awaken, heal, and improve the quality of their lives.

I know your vision is bigger than your current results. My promise with this book is to help you fulfill your greatest purpose and mission. As a healer-coach, you are guided to deliver your mission on earth. Whether it's as an earth angel, a goddess, a warrior, or a healer-empath, you're here to shift paradigms and the game. My seven hacks will accelerate this path, make it easier and more enjoyable, and create the flow that will enable you to express your genius.

Through my 7 Quantum Hacks, you will be able to make simple shifts and hit reset on your life and healer-coach business forever. That means no more time-consuming self-development classes to reunite you with your mojo. No awful credit card investments to keep your business afloat. No workshops, seminars, or retreats where the minute you get home, you're yanked back to a reality far away from the bliss you felt only in the moment. Trust me, I've been there.

Rewire Upwire

Many people downwire as they age, but it doesn't have to be that way. When you lean into possibilities and become different with the intention to get better, you are "Upwiring." The key to upgrading your performance is to spend the majority of your time Upwiring rather than downwiring.

Dave Asprey, *Game Changers: What Leaders, Innovators, and Mavericks Do to Win at Life*

As you may know, our primary mode of brain functioning in the world today is the performance code of two thousand years ago. As many profound self-development teachers have stated, our instinct is to get up in the morning and repeat exactly what we did the day before. This is a survival mechanism of the brain that is associated with staying alive. The brain is here to keep you alive. However, this is a primitive, amygdala-based mode of functioning. In order to evolve beyond this mode of functioning, we need to either upgrade or rewire the survival-brain functioning and move into an upwiring mode. But how do we do this, you may be wondering.

The whole world goes in the direction of the survival mode of functioning, with the emphasis on fear, surrounding us in the messages of the media. You can try to override this primitive functioning at will. Most self-help and law-of-attraction gurus would have you repeat affirmations that you don't believe and attend events that do not impact you when you return home to your normal routine. So how do you rewire and upwire the daily, minute-to-minute level of functioning of your brain?

What the Heck Does "Quantum" Mean?

Those who are not shocked when they first come across quantum theory cannot possibly have understood it.

Niels Bohr
recipient of the 1922 Nobel Prize in
Physics for his work on the structure
of the atom quoted in *Physics and Beyond*
by Werner Heisenberg

The term *quantum* was first applied to science by the German physicist Max Planck in 1900. It is a Latin word that simply means "amount" or "quantity," but it is used to mean the smallest unit of any physical property, such as energy or matter. In this sense, *quantum* means subatomic particles, and *quantum theory* studies how these subatomic particles behave. *Quanta* are the smallest particles in the universe.

The mystery of these subatomic particles confounds even the most sophisticated scientist. For example, a subatomic particle can appear in three thousand places at once.

As anesthesiologist Dr. Stuart Hameroff states, at the small-scale level of atoms, a different set of laws takes over. These are quantum laws. When we speak of energy waves and frequencies, we are describing something that impacts the flow of life and our very existence on the subatomic level; this can impact your reality in mysterious ways.

If you are fascinated by this and would like to delve more deeply into the quantum mysteries, I recommend the movie and book *What the Bleep Do We Know!?* by William Arntz, Betsy Chasse, and Mark Vicente.

The only premise you need to understand is that we are frequency and vibration, and that these fundamental frequencies emitted by our brain can be rewired, upwired, upgraded, altered, supported, and optimized efficiently by sound waves. Dave Asprey, the "father of biohacking" and author of *Game Changers*, coined the term *upwiring* to describe how a field of quantum sound waves can do this. When bathing in this field of quantum sound waves, your personal brain waves automatically align with the beneficial and soothing sound waves vibrating in the environment. Throughout this book, I will use Dave Asprey's word *upwire* and neuroscience's word *rewire*. These words have the same meaning.

Keep in mind that this book condenses over thirty-five years of my experience, and forty-five years of my partner Robert Lloy's experience, in the realms of quantum sound technology, personal growth, and therapy. I present our condensed years of experience and research in the 7 Quantum Hacks.

More Than Brain Wave Entrainment

The process through which our brain can upwire and optimize by following sound waves is called *brain wave entrainment*. Brain wave entrainment is any practice, tool, or technology that aims to cause brain wave frequencies to align with an external stimulus. When we experience specific frequencies, we align with them and alter our brain wave state.

What I am describing here in this book, *Quantum Sound Miracle iQube,* is more profound than mere brain wave entrainment, as it involves another dimension of the dynamic quantum field. Consider it as a continual flow of electronic feng shui that continually clears and uplifts both your energy field and your environment, while sending messages in the form of harmonious sound waves to upgrade your moment-to-moment experience of life.

The technology allows you to eat cake and lose weight at the same time, the best of both worlds.

Some of these are audible frequencies; some are inaudible, being in a range of delta that humans cannot hear. However, with our unique waveform, in which we integrate six waveforms to beat together, even some of the delta frequencies become audible.

The quantum sound field is being generated 24-7; these highly beneficial sound waves are automatically and continuously received by your brain. Think of it as a tuning fork that continues to vibrate, balance, and harmonize your energy field even while you are sleeping. When two tuning forks are near each other and one is struck so that it vibrates, in short order the second tuning fork begins to vibrate in resonance. We are like tuning forks. We automatically resonate and vibrate in tune with these beneficial sound waves. We find ourselves releasing lower vibrations and resonating with coherent vibrations.

The principle of resonance is automatic, effortless, and continuous. With our Quantum Sound field, you are swimming in a highly coherent, uplifting field that you do not need to do anything to maintain.

The environmental cleansing effect is similar to activating a Roomba robot vacuum that never stops working or clearing. It is like having a proficient energy healer clearing your environment and your field continuously, and delivering the most uplifting gong bath or tuning-fork therapy session. Unlike with the temporary gong bath or tuning-fork meditation, these frequencies are delivered continually. Only a power outage or not paying your electric bill will stop these harmonious, uplifting sound waves from being both delivered and received.

These sound waves work on both your environment and your personal field, and on all other inhabitants who share the field with you. Even if someone enters the field only temporarily, they will benefit. Sound uplifting? It is. Sound out of the box? It is.

The future of healing is when we transition to a reality that impacts our whole environment. It is for this reason that many healer-coaches have called our work a new support system, or a best friend. For me, it's the gift that keeps on giving.

Does It Sound Too Good to Be True?

As everything is frequency, you can alter the frequency of your environment by adding sound waves. Some people are sensitive enough to feel this shift immediately.

You probably already know about this if you have heard of *binaural beats,* in which two different tones are played simultaneously, one in each ear, resulting in your brain hearing the intervening tone. But what if I said you can extend this theory to something far more sophisticated than binaural music? What I am alluding to is an approach at an entirely new level. It is to prepare for the new vibrations that are arriving here on earth now. The Quantum Sound Miracle system will support and facilitate your move from Human 1.0 to Human 2.0 fluidly. These sound waves create coherence in the environment and in your brain wave patterns.

The Game Changer

In the words of Marci Shimoff, *New York Times* bestselling author, transformational leader, motivational expert, and author of the foreword to this book,

> *I had spent my lifetime doing personal development work and meditation. Some of the deepest blocks that I had not been able to deal with came up and were resolved in the first three weeks of having the* [Quantum Sound Therapy iQube] *in my home and office.*

Marci found she was integrating miracles into her coaching and consulting business.

Let me give you another example. One coach approached me with a relationship issue, a fear of intimacy. Although she had spent hundreds of thousands of dollars hiring a variety of well-known personal-development coaches over a few years, she was still stuck—until she installed the Quantum Sound Therapy system in her home.

Easily, her issue with intimacy and relationships released.

Within four weeks, this lovely client went on to meet the love of her life; four weeks after beginning to use this modality, she was engaged. Through the release, and therefore the resolution of her frequency blocks at the subconscious level, her underlying fear of intimacy shifted. Her frequency allowed her to manifest from a place of openness and acceptance, and she was quickly able to attract a compatible partner who was attracted to her raised vibrations.

From a quantum viewpoint, there is no space and time in the continuum, just consciousness and acts of creation.

To access quantum sound healing, you don't even need to leave your home or office. In fact, you'll love being there even more! Now, when you book a flight to an exotic destination, it won't be to see the inside of a windowless ballroom for the next healing workshop. You'll be able to enjoy the tropics from the highest of vibrations with the ultimate in energetic states.

You're smart. You've mastered your healer-coach modality. Of course you have. You are passionate about delivering great service and keen to see even better results. Whether it's acupuncture, Reiki, massage, life coaching, health coaching, kinesiology, hypnosis, or any other of the hundreds of approaches to healing, there has always been something missing. Am I right?

Answer this: how much energy does it take for you to remain in your current state? Remember that even Tony Robbins's coaches put a lot of effort into getting into an optimal state before working with a coaching client on the phone. I have fast routes that require little or no focus.

In the coming chapters, you will read stories of transformation featuring well-known scientists and bestselling authors and speakers, as well as inspiring changes that the average person does not know are possible. These frequency-based tales confirm my life's work and purpose to transform, uplift, and upwire. They include stories about Dr. Masaru Emoto;

Tony Robbins; Mike Reilly, my son; an accountant who called to report that his client had spent $50,000 on self-development courses, a child on the autism spectrum who returned to normal classrooms; an alcoholic who spontaneously stopped drinking; the brain researcher Octavio Pino, MD; and the *New York Times* bestselling author of six books in the Chicken Soup series, Marci Shimoff.

I'm going to reveal some quantum secrets now:

✓ The missing ingredient in your healer-coach business lies in the challenge of continually managing your resonance and the sound vibrations of your energy field and body, of your client's energy field and body, and of the environment.

✓ The second blind spot (and by far the most important to this book) is that you are missing a modality that efficiently detects, addresses, and releases the deeply embedded patterns of the subconscious mind that are running the show. Once the content of the subconscious is pinpointed and released, all other modalities that you have studied and are applying will have far greater potency.

Everything is frequency and vibration, and when this frequency is harmonized and aligned, we return to peace and prosperity. Through the manipulation of quantum sound frequencies, you can rewire and upwire your frequency so that it's optimized for the present and the future—not for two thousand years ago, as author Dave Asprey points out. You can also upwire the actual field of your environment (both home and office) so that it works to uplift your frequency whether you are consciously aware of it or not—for instance, during your sleep cycle.

At times, some of my concepts may read like the elements of an elaborate sci-fi novel. I'm here to reveal and prove that once you grasp these quantum concepts, you can implement them, along with the relevant technology. Through resonance shifts, it's possible to naturally and effortlessly clear energetic debris, such as our environmental challenges. It may seem that electromagnetic fields (EMFs) are one of the largest outputs of disruptive energy. We live together in an environment—a subtle energy field—that is constantly being affected by invisible waves of energy: EMFs, dirty electricity (erratic spikes of energy higher than 60 hertz), artificial lighting, and sound waves. We entrain with this field consciously and subconsciously.

These harmful effects can be shifted as well. With the right technology and comprehension, even the dense and engulfing rays emanating from our ever-increasing number of handheld devices can be transmuted out of harm's way.

You and I are distinct fields of frequency and vibration. Each of us has a brain that emits its personal energetic signature. We also entrain with the personal energetic signatures of other people. Think, for example, of your best friend who visits you and stays with you in your home. She is depressed. You feel this. You are now empathizing and entraining with her field.

If you had the Quantum Sound Miracle iQube vibrating its scalar wave essence in your home or office, the beneficial field would automatically massage and uplift your friend, so you would not have to do as much of the heavy lifting. She would raise her energy to the sound waves. You would both benefit from the quantum sound therapy.

All extraneous energies can be cleared 24-7—all the time!—to clear a path to the sensation of complete wellness and the joy that accompanies this abundant energy within the body. You pass your increased vibrations on to your clients through the principle of resonance.

Through brain wave entrainment, your effectiveness—no matter your primary modality as a healer-coach—will exponentially increase. Whether your brain is retrained during waking hours or through delta waves during sleep, the results show an increase in productivity, clarity, and creativity. It's like someone turns the dial up to high on all you have been practicing, so you're no longer slow-baking everything you do.

When you're in the process of raising the frequency of your personal and environmental energy fields, there is no set order to follow. The only wrong way to hack your energy field, and to support your clients doing so, is to not do it at all. Trust me, I know and see people who are stuck in an unproductive modality.

Each chapter works as a complete approach to integrating these upgrades in one easy plug-and-play. The smart world that you create will automatically discharge your field, your environment, and your clients' fields, effortlessly. This new world integrates a zero-point field into your life. Zero point is a pure state that exists before thought, before matter, before time. The Quantum Sound Therapy system is a new way to integrate a zero-point field into your life. Once you reach zero point, you're freed up to follow your passions wholly and allow your rock-star brilliance to shine through. It's like getting a royal security detail so you can carry on with your life's mission without interference.

I invite you to read on if you resonate with learning more about these breakthrough concepts all rolled into one plug-and-play technology.

You've found me and you resonate with what I'm saying. Stick with me on this epic journey of vibrational discovery, and you'll learn about

1. The science-based quantum sound technology that allows you to generate ongoing higher vibrations in your home and practice, elevating all output from that space.
2. A breakthrough voice-based modality that detects and releases your subconscious blocks.
3. A way to activate your seat of genius, for increased focus, productivity, and in turn, prosperity.
4. Awakening your intuition.
5. Deeper, longer, more productive delta sleep and dreaming cycles, for a day charged with energy and focus.
6. Imbibing high-frequency structured water and food to raise your cellular vibrational matrix.
7. Getting off the emotional roller-coaster ride of seeking harmony and balance externally.

Might This Be Helpful for You and Your Clients?

It's easy to acknowledge that you have blocks holding you back, but how can you identify what they are when they are resonating at a subtle, subconscious level? On a frequency level, they may eliminate themselves over time, but how can you intentionally alter and improve energetic vibrations?

Engage with this missing modality. I know—I've seen it frequently, firsthand. A healer-coach will gain the power to change her own life and business and become a catalyst for change in her clients' lives. Through this technology, every night you hit your own personal reset button, through deep delta sleep and lucid dreaming, so that you process the unwelcome subconscious programming from the day and awake refreshed and aligned with your soul-spirit consciousness.

I will share the science-based precision modalities that will improve the bottom line of your healing business while transforming your daily experience as a holistic business owner forever! I'm here to help you access your inner rock star and set yourself free so that the world benefits from your gifts.

Now let's explore the magic ingredients, so you can take back your healer mojo, raise your frequency, and help your clients attain new levels of transformation, well-being, and happiness!

If you're ready to take back your mojo, read on!

PART II

These are the 7 Quantum Hacks I'll describe in Part II:

- ✓ Hack 1: Quantum Clearing
- ✓ Hack 2: Quantum Attuning
- ✓ Hack 3: Quantum Activating
- ✓ Hack 4: Quantum Awakening
- ✓ Hack 5: Quantum Repatterning
- ✓ Hack 6: Quantum Imprinting
- ✓ Hack 7: Quantum Awareness

CHAPTER 4

Hack 1:
Superhero Sanctuary

The Subtle Field of Energy
We Are Swimming In

*Isn't it ironic, then, that we keep all of our attention on the
0.00001 percent of reality that is physical? Are we missing
something?*

Joe Dispenza,
Breaking the Habit of Being Yourself

*I*f I could promise you a peaceful bubble in your home and
office—a superhero sanctuary that envelops you in high
vibrations that would automatically raise your frequency
(upwire you), enhance your intuition, and bring you greater
peace, harmony, and clarity—would you be interested?

Maybe you don't realize how the field of energy you are
unconsciously swimming in is dragging you down.

You may be thinking this sounds too good to be true.
Beyond your wildest dreams. You may be asking, "How can I
do this, living in this insanely busy and distracting world?"

In this chapter I am going to share a very new approach that will pave a pathway to enhancing your ability and potential in every dimension of your life. Mind you, it has taken a lifetime to develop this approach. Hack 1 is the creation of a field of quantum energy that heals your environment so that you can exist in an enlivened state continuously.

Once you experience this consciousness and concept, you will begin to thrive instead of just survive in your daily life. You will no longer find it necessary to escape and chase self-development gurus all over planet earth, because you will automatically become your own guru, and your expanded intuition will become your guide.

First, let's establish the foundation.

Your environment consists of energy waves that carry information to your brain, body, and energy field continually. This is the field of energy that you are swimming in. Most of this field remains unseen and unheard. It is received unconsciously into your field. It is being transmitted to you day and night.

The Quantum Field of Potential

Your interaction with this field occurs primarily on an unconscious level. You have invisible radar, like an antenna, that automatically picks up information from this energy field. You are like a cell tower that picks up the radio frequency waves and transmits them; you receive this information continuously and unconsciously.

The frequency of the information you pick up has far greater impact on your health and well-being than you are consciously aware of. Yes, this field even impacts your digestion!

As a field of energy, your brain is constantly seeking and acquiring new information on all levels of your awareness. Your brain seeks new information from the environment to entrain with. Entraining is an advanced and subtle form of unconscious learning that goes on continuously every moment of your life, whether you are sleeping or awake. As a matter of fact, according to the genius neuroscientist and neurolinguist Octavio Pino, MD, the brain is actually more receptive while sleeping or in the restorative delta brain wave state.

I still remember quite clearly the day Dr. Pino explained this to me and the light bulb went on. Dr. Octavio Pino is a mystic, a brain researcher, and a neurolinguist who speaks seven languages fluently. He clearly explained how the brain is actually a field of information that is continually seeking new information.

Envision your expanded brain as a field, now seeking some new information in Africa or on the internet.

Take a moment. Close your eyes and visualize an antenna at the top of your head. This may seem a little silly at first. The antenna acts to receive information and frequencies. It is searching for a signal. Once it receives this signal, your chemistry, mood, and emotions are unconsciously altered.

Does it make sense to you, then, to refer to this invisible and yet powerful field as a quantum field of invisible intelligence that continually instructs you and everyone else in your environment?

Does it make sense that this field is invisibly governing your law of attraction?

Does it make sense to alter this, or to design this field in an intelligent way so that you are growing in consciousness while you sleep, eat, and meditate?

Does it make further sense that by increasing the energy and quality of the information you are picking up (imbibing) from your environment, you can actually enhance your abilities and the quality of your life—naturally and forever?

Energy Waves and Tiny Packets of Information

Let me ask you this question: if the environment consists of energy waves that carry tiny packets of information, and this very energy informs our environment, our body, and our brain continuously, does it make sense to you to design this information, up-level it and upwire it so that it feeds your consciousness good stuff instead of junk food?

Then, to take it one step further, does it not make sense to design the instruction on a subtle level? We certainly do this with all of the visible, physical aspects of our lives. We design our homes and the food we feed our bodies.

I'm going to drive this point home.

We design every external aspect of our lives that we can see. We design our homes intentionally to enhance our well-being. We use feng shui, sage, incense, and the like to "clear discordant energies." You can just watch one episode from a series of millionaire real estate agents in Malibu to see the extent of this obsession. We design our cars, our diet, our clothing, our noses, our exercise routines, our yoga and meditation clothing, our summer vacations, the schools and colleges we send our children to, and even our buttocks, as you can see by the recent popularity of the Brazilian butt lift.

Everything we can see, we design. And yet this activity that takes all of our energy is trying to design and enhance less than one percent of our reality, according to the experts, for instance, neuroscientist and author Joe Dispenza.

So, what about designing the subtle energy of the field we are surrounded by, imbibing unconsciously, and swimming in?

If we don't design this aspect of our existence, we are no different than fish swimming in water that is so heavily polluted that it will result in their demise. We are unconsciously swimming in dirty energy. And with the advent of fifth-generation cellular network technology (5G), this energy field is about to become far more entangling, complex, and dense. We are entangled in a field that we are almost completely unaware of.

The most recent brain researchers and consciousness experts are calling the attempt to intentionally raise the frequency of our consciousness *upwiring*. (I write about this in chapter 3.) The goal is to design ways to feed the brain conscious information that naturally uplifts, rewires, and upwires our functioning.

Does this make sense to you?

Since energy organizes itself in some way or another into matter, if we somehow hack the information, will the matter—in this case your brain, consciousness, vibration, and energy field—change? Alter? Adapt? Can you raise your frequency and optimize your healing results and life by designing the subtle energy field of your environment? Would this then become your fortress of solitude?

The Shift from the External to the Internal Search

I'm going to share an anecdote to drive this point home.

This story is about a person who went outside of themselves (external vibration upliftment and upwiring) to attend personal-development events in order to orchestrate a change of state. We call these workshops, conferences, conventions, or summits.

The environment at these events is always carefully designed so that the participants experience a high, a break-through, a feeling of equanimity and expansion. The environments are designed to make you feel that you are invincible, you can do anything, and you will realize your quantum potential in an instant.

People become easily addicted to this experience of an altered field and return many times to receive this energy. This person ended up in severe credit card debt for attending such events, and it was the family accountant who realized this had become a form of addiction that was bankrupting the family's financial future, possibly impacting their ability to retire.

There is very powerful evidence that confirms that it is more powerful to design and alter the field of your own home and office space to support you on your quantum journey than to continually seek upliftment outside yourself. When we design our environment, it raises the frequency and operates to uplift our energy field.

$50,000 Call from an Accountant

You can imagine my surprise when I received the phone call from that accountant—his name is Bill—asking for my help. His client, a woman in her mid-fifties—let's call her Lisa—had been spending in excess of $50,000 a year, traveling to exotic locations at five-star hotels and retreats to participate in various self-development events orchestrated by different gurus.

Whether it was a certification she was acquiring, a meditation intensive, or an intense drug-induced spiritual journey, like partaking of ayahuasca, Lisa was trying it all. So much so that she had amassed credit card debt that alarmed her accountant, Bill. Lisa had no intention of slowing down these self-development excursions, because she was addicted to the high vibe she experienced during these events. These adventures would energize her in their field of high vibration and emotions. She made new friends and she was able to get her mojo back in order to continue to cope with the daily challenges of her life, her business, and her marriage.

The effects of the high, however, were simply not lasting. She would remain in bliss for perhaps three days, until she crashed and found herself in the zone of struggle again. Sound familiar? I call this the roller-coaster ride of emotional ups and downs: struggling to get through the day or to deal with yet another problem or issue, struggling to find that intuitive inspiration to help her clients, struggling to find her center. Just plain struggling to find her own genius zone and enjoy her daily life. And also, to add the icing on the cake, struggling to cope with mounting credit card debt.

The accountant was not just concerned about the $50,000 in wellness spending. Lisa's husband was about to retire on a pension, and together the couple had little in the way of savings or investments. Bill's call came as a desperate plea for me to assist in shifting this addictive pattern. Yes, even though it was all personal development work, it was showing up in her life to fill a void.

Lisa had a small energy healing business in Southern California. She felt bombarded by the emotional ups and downs that accompanied hot flashes and hormonal imbalances. She was an empty-nester, with both her children in college.

Lisa's husband was perplexed. He could not understand why she was so invested in these domestic and international workshops. He asked himself what was missing from her life that she felt this urge to continually escape, and he wondered why her work was so energetically challenging that she had to frequently escape it, and her home environment, to reset. He had spoken to Bill, the accountant, with concerns beyond the financial, questioning whether she was unhappy in the marriage or having an affair. Neither Bill nor Lisa's husband could fathom her behavior, nor could the couple continue to financially support such a habit, with retirement looming.

I was glad Bill had called me. I understood things from all perspectives! As I was clear on the concept of all things quantum being in an empty space, I was able to carefully explain that it was not a void she was filling.

Lisa was not a fool to travel to enlighten herself. She was experiencing new fields of energy that she found uplifting to her body, mind, and spirit. She was traveling to make new connections, both within herself and with like-minded others. She was traveling to entrain in a positive energy field that was consciously created by the leader, teacher, or guide hosting the event. That $50,000 expense was a quantum investment! She was diversely expanding her innate neuroplastic capability—but it was innate. It was her inner real estate resource to expand. Therefore, she had the option to attain the same results with a different process.

In chapter 3, I explained about the zero-point field. There are plenty of external places that people like Lisa seek out where they can connect with enlightening new energy fields.

But, as I explained to Bill, my work has taken that search from an external to an internal place. I explained that my life-work and business has focused on the creation of tools and technologies that generate a zero-point quantum field of energy in your own space—home, office, or even hotel. While Lisa would be sad to let an exotic destination or two fall off her calendar, the opportunity to receive automatic training consistently, instead of sporadically at these events, was a measure of success for everyone involved.

How would this shift from the external to the internal be accomplished? Through sound wave entrainment. I explained to Bill that we could achieve the same results for Lisa, but with greater stability, by focusing on tools and technologies that automatically entrain you into higher vibrational states from your present space. These vibrational tools and technologies act like a tuning fork to re-establish clarity and balance in your life.

When the conversation moved in this direction, Bill became interested.

Lisa isn't unique in seeking out peak upgrade moments, when she can become aligned with her higher self, encouraging a sense of an overall uplift alongside a like-minded community seeking something extraordinary. These states, however, could easily be experienced by alignment with frequencies that would uplift and transform her state even while she slept. Or in her office when she is booked solid with clients who are filled with emotional aches and physical pains.

Lisa is just like most of us. She knew what it felt like to hit the reset button and raise her frequency. It felt just wonderful to her. It was the flow state: the inevitable joy of being in flow, in the moment, in a beautiful, expansive environment with like-minded soul friends. It was like a real celebration, not a calculated one. She was impacted positively by an increase in vibration at these events. Lisa's external search was to resonate in a bandwidth that could help her shift, awaken, relax, and become inspired again. I know you've been there—at a seminar, in front of a spiritual leader, on a retreat—which is why I decided to share this work with you.

Every time Lisa intuited that her body was vibrating out of harmony, she would seek another fix. A quick web search and the click of a "buy now" button, and she'd find herself booked into another external event to recalibrate her back to wholeness.

This is my first hack, my first shared secret after thirty-five years of research.

Like Lisa, you too can solve your energetic and emotional instabilities by creating an uplifting fortress of solitude—in both your home and your office. This will act as your energetic sanctuary.

When you have a haven in which to attune yourself back to a higher frequency, you make the decision to attend those external events optional, not a necessity.

While Bill began to understand my message, I could see there was a need to provide a real-life example of success in this area. I shared another story that I will now share with you: my tale from my former clients, Chris and Irene, and the tangible power of energetic changes to consciousness.

"Where's the Master Hiding?"

Chris and Irene host weekly meditation sessions at their home in San Diego, and always have some very seasoned meditators present. Here's what happened at one of their evening meditation sessions, when my Quantum Sound Miracle technology was humming in the background.

During the session, a seasoned meditator entered their home and immediately tuned into the energetically enhanced field. She asked Chris and Irene, "Where is the master hiding?"

Chris explained that there was no master present but that they were running my quantum sound technology, the Quantum Sound Miracle iQube.

Like Lisa, the student was familiar with workshops and retreats in the presence of masters, and she could not attribute this energetic flow to technology. Recognizing being in the presence of an elevated quantum field of energy, the student's conscious and subconscious mind recognized the power and coherence of this energy field, which was emitting alpha, theta, and delta frequencies. She could only associate these increased vibrations with the sensations she had felt in the presence of an enlightened soul. She felt certain that Chris and Irene were hiding a master somewhere in their home, and even proceeded to search the entire house looking for the master-in-hiding. She even searched the closets, the bedrooms, and under the bed!

Sans monk, guru, or master in the field, she finally accepted that what they were saying was the truth. She was tuning into the quantum energy field generated by the sound technology of the iQube.

Depending on where you are in your own journey, you may have sensed these vibrational shifts in the presence of masters, on visits to sacred sites and vortexes, or even at simple gatherings. No matter what aligned you with this higher frequency, you've subconsciously felt this. *Resonance* refers to the way we each naturally vibrate in tune with an object or a person, at their specific frequency. Every object and every person has a resonant frequency. Everything is in a state of constant vibration, including the body.

Chris and Irene understood the benefits of being in the presence of an enhanced energetic field, enough to invest in the technology to enhance their practice. The student's connection to a "master's energy" only enhanced what they knew to be true. And if Lisa's husband and accountant had been able to understand that the events she attended had acted as a tuning fork for her vibrations and resonance in her body, mind, and spirit, they might have begun to appreciate the addictive connection with greater clarity after hearing this story. I explained to Bill that Lisa's seeking a state of well-being was a beautiful thing. And that yes, there are alternative ways to work with your vibration and to generate a field that is positive and uplifting.

Lisa's situation is very familiar to me. I've met with countless clients who are striving for increased resonance, only to experience the roller-coaster ride of emotional ups and downs.

I answered the accountant's plea affirmatively. I could assist Lisa to design the energy, support, and comfort she was seeking. This field would encourage her to return to her own source of power rather than seeking it at external events.

Resonant Frequency Healing

I can assist healers and coaches through my quantum sound technology, generating powerful quantum fields that act as tuning forks to automatically entrain consciousness into an inevitable state of coherent well-being. Those present effortlessly experience shifts in awareness and consciousness that are elevating, uplifting, and detoxing.

However, there exist more efficient, cost-effective ways to find this state of flow and to align with it more frequently, so that a healer's life and her business can thrive.

Through the principles of entrainment, these quantum fields are so powerful that they are capable of creating huge shifts in all manners of behavior, including addictions of all types.

All the great masters of self-development understand that entrainment is an important principle of vibrational cleansing and upgrading. Entrainment occurs naturally. The key to healing through entrainment is the sound wave attracting our frequency-following response. When we are subjected to specific frequencies, we align with this and alter our brain wave state.

When you join a master or self-development leader, you, along with their tribe of followers, make a decision to entrain with their resonance. You admire these leaders. You resonate with them, and as a result you entrain with their frequency. Their tribe of followers joins up with them periodically to entrain with the resonance of the leader. This gives the student the temporary lift in vibration associated with entrainment. When you leave the energetic fortress they have carefully curated, you experience a natural drop in your frequency. This may materialize as a feeling of letdown, emptiness, sadness, or even, more dramatically, a sense of falling off a cliff into an abyss. I have heard students say, "Nothing seems to fit anymore. I don't want to go back to my job or my husband."

Or it may simply be that you sense a drop in your emotions, the equivalent of passing through the big dip on a roller coaster. Typically, these events cover a long weekend, which in my experience is too short to adequately embody the increased resonance to a maintainable level. They give you a hit of elevated frequency but not lasting, permanent change. It is like rehearsing a play once and expecting mastery. There is just not enough immersion in the process to attain the desired result or outcome.

Entraining within Your Designer Fortress of Solitude

Entrainment is a phenomenon of sound in which the powerful vibrations of one object change those of another, causing the second object to synchronize with the first. You may not be conscious of it, but we undergo entrainment frequently, adapting and shifting with different external vibrations that we are surrounded by. A good example of this is when we go to the beach. We are in nature, and the waves are gently rolling to shore. We entrain with this beautiful rhythm of the waves and the sea. Entraining with this rhythmic pattern is very different from entraining with, for example, the hustle bustle of New York City.

We also experience this with our internal rhythms. For example, with our heartbeats, our breathing, and our brain wave activity. We will entrain with others' patterns and rhythms, such as with a newborn baby lying on our stomach when we are its parent. We entrain with the baby's calming frequency of love. And it goes the other way. If, for example, a mother is anxious, the baby may become colicky.

Let's experiment with this. Take a few deep breaths into your belly, the deepest breaths you'll have taken today. As you slow down your respiration, you'll be able to notice the influence this has on your heart rate. You'll no doubt feel calmer with these breaths, which is also a demonstration of the entrainment of your brain waves.

The Brain as a Field of Energy

What you need to understand here is that your brain is not just a physical organ. It is an electrochemical organ, a nonphysical field of energy that radiates brain waves like beta, alpha, theta, gamma, and delta. Its electricity is measured in brain waves.

Through my own studies, I have experienced firsthand the complexity of the brain's energy field and how it is always in search of new information. It produces electromagnetic frequencies that can be measured in a way very similar to how we measure sound: in cycles per second, or hertz (Hz). Of course, sound frequencies can influence our brain wave patterns.

Distinct brain wave activity is correlated with a spectrum of frequencies known as *brain wave states*, which go from 0.5 Hz to 20 Hz. You will probably have heard of terms like *alpha brain waves*, *beta brain waves*, and *theta brain waves*.

Through consistent entrainment, your brain wave patterns can be altered and enhanced, and with that upwiring, your behavioral patterns and energetic field automatically transform too. These changes occur throughout the day and even when you're sleeping. In fact, especially when you're sleeping. It is in this delta wave state, according to Dr. Octavio Pino, that the brain is the most receptive to new information. I will share more on this in chapter 8.

Let me give you the basic lowdown on the five categories of brain waves, ranging from the fastest to the slowest, so you understand the tools that allow you to upwire your brain. An interesting fast fact: the quickest brain waves correspond with lower-frequency awareness, while the slowest brain waves correlate with higher frequencies and expanded awareness.

Could Gamma Brain Waves Be the Tuning Fork of the Divine?

Gamma brain waves have the fastest frequency, at between 30 and 100-plus Hz, and the smallest amplitude. They are associated with the feelings of blessings, oneness, and bliss reported by experienced meditators, such as monks and nuns. Gamma waves are associated with peak performance concentration and high levels of cognitive functioning. I realized that the masters I have lived with spend a significant amount of time in gamma brain wave states and theta brain wave states.

Neuroscientists believe that gamma waves are able to link information from all parts of the brain. You could envision the whole brain lighting up.

The gamma wave originates in the thalamus, and moves from the back of the brain to the front and back again forty times per second. This rapid "full sweep" action makes the gamma state one of peak mental and physical performance. Gamma is the brainwave state of being "in the zone."

Everyone has gamma brainwave activity, but the amount of gamma waves produced in each person varies. Low amounts of gamma brainwave activity have been linked to learning difficulties, poor memory, and impaired mental processing.

What Do Gamma Binaural Beats Do?

Gamma binaural beats are shown to **positively affect our memory**, and can even slow certain medical conditions, such as Alzheimer's disease.

How? Well, Alzheimer's disease is the result of plaque (beta-amyloid) building up between our neurons. Scientists believe that gamma waves positively impact our immunity by telling our immune system to attack this disease-causing plaque.

Beta, Alpha, Theta, and Delta Brain Waves

At between 13 and 40 Hz, beta is the next fastest of the brain waves. It is associated with an alert waking state, when your brain is aroused and engaged in mental activity. An example of low beta would be when you read in bed before sleep; high beta occurs around intense activity or arousal. The energy from a theme park often puts us in a state of high beta—whether it's from being surprised on ghost train, feeling fear on the loop-the-loop, or being hungry as you line up for fairground food.

Alpha brain waves are slower, from 8 to 13 Hz. They appear when you're relaxed but not drowsy. This is during an effortless period of alertness, such as during light meditation, reflection, daydreaming, and body-mind integration. Alpha is also experienced during light hypnosis, creative visualization, and artistic and intuitive processes, as well as when we spend time in nature. Most meditation recordings enhance entrainment with the alpha wave state.

Theta brain waves, from 4 to 8 Hz, are much slower and are associated with the first stage of sleep, drowsiness, dreaming, deeper levels of meditation, and inspired creativity. Perhaps you can recall this from a time of creative flow, when you felt like you were almost in a trance as inspiration flowed. During theta, you have heightened imagination, increased recall, and seemingly mystical states of intuition. Have you ever felt the inspiration of a brilliant idea or vision during a long shower or on a familiar drive home? That's theta, and it can often accompany a feeling of having lost track of time.

Delta, at 0.5 to 4 Hz, is a period of very slow brain waves. Delta occurs during deep sleep, and this is the state when you are able to "repattern," reprogram, release, and heal. When your brain is in delta, you're at your most receptive to the information and the frequencies emitted by the quantum sound technology. Deep delta is associated with deep trance states and processes of self-healing.

Your brain shifts between these four basic frequencies of consciousness, beta, alpha, theta, and delta. At each vibratory level, you function differently. These phases are evident during your sleep cycle. At night, you rotate through several phases of sleep. In the early stage, your brain waves slow from beta to the more relaxed alpha state.

So how does the positive alteration of the field of your environment impact you?

The quantum field is composed of empty particles of information that are actually seeking to be filled or informed with new information. Let's look at this as though it is empty space. Unfortunately, most of us fill our quantum field of unlimited potential with repetitive behaviors, thoughts, and emotions. Whether it's a contrary habit, a dismissive response, or a hostile pattern, that negative energy exudes a downward vibratory level, an ineffectual use of our intelligence and behavior. Of course, there are countless self-development books, courses, and workshops that want you to extract yourself from these negative energy flows, but this requires time-consuming effort. By employing my 7 Quantum Hacks, you can extricate lowered frequency waves from the body, mind, and your environment. It's like lifting a heavy backpack from your back on a hundred-mile hike—but I can help you walk without the backpack at all.

On a scientific level, here is what unfolds when unlimited quantum potential shifts into a solid form and manifests as tangible **results**. You automatically reset from state A (let's say, for example, on the autism spectrum) to state B (enjoying all normal classrooms and entering school as a chef). The results can be dramatic when the energy is repatterned or reorganized. Trust me on this one. I hear about it every day! You are then in the 2.0 version of yourself.

This unlimited quantum potential is organized and downloaded from energy to subatomic particles and then creates everything we see—the body, the mind, the environment. It actually lowers the frequency of wave patterns until it appears as a solid form.

Each story illustrates an aspect of how, when you design your space to be filled with coherent energy and information that cultivates your own fortress of solitude, anything is possible. You have a far greater likelihood of spontaneously breaking the habit of being yourself—transforming your repetitive behavior and emotional patterns without so much heavy lifting or the high cost associated with it. I felt these stories illustrated this, so I'm calling them "straight outta quantum," to borrow a term from my dear friend Jessica Alstrom, quantum life coach, medical intuitive, and quantum sound healer. The quantum coherent field that you are generating is doing the heavy lifting, which is why clients say that it is like having the heaviness just lifted away.

I am going to tell you three stories to clarify the hack of designing the energetics of the environment with quantum sound to work for you 24-7, while you work, eat, play, and relax.

"Straight Outta Quantum"

Optimizing Your Field of Genius

I described in chapter 1 how Tony Robbins's personal assistant called three nights before Christmas 2018 to purchase a Quantum Sound Miracle iQube for Tony and his wife Sage. Of course, they wanted the Miracle as soon as possible. Not only had the Miracle creation team in Hot Springs, Arkansas, gone home for the Christmas holidays, but the Miracle was in backorder status. The Miracles are like custom pieces of art—we create them by hand one at a time.

Who doesn't want a Christmas Miracle? Fortunately, I always have a demo unit running at the side of my desk, so I offered to ship this to them, with an agreement that we would replace the unit with a brand new Miracle in the new year.

After receiving the Miracle, Sage called with some detailed questions and asked if I would be able to meet the Robbins team at their home to answer a few questions.

What I realized during our uplifting meeting was that Tony and Sage understood the profound significance and impact of the subtle energy field in their home; it was assisting them to get "in state." They had reached out to us because they had the desire and vision to maintain a high-vibrating energetic force field in their home, beyond their own magnanimous efforts.

They were seeking a clear vortex, free from negative or lowered emotional states, a field that would enhance their co-creative genius while deepening their sleep and meditation. Of course they have many practices and tools to maintain their energy and their state, which is so impressive! They intuitively understood the process of maintaining the highest vibration in their home and were seeking an understanding of the shortcuts we had implemented through the Quantum Sound Miracle. What a joy and a pleasure that "straight outta quantum" afternoon was, two days after Christmas.

If you know anything about Tony Robbins's work, you'll know he wants to remain in a high vibrational state so he can fulfill his mission to serve as many people at the highest level possible. And he intuitively knew that he had found a subtle way to support the energy field—so much so that he purchased nine Quantum iQubes at the conclusion of our meeting!

At that moment, I saw that we were evolving toward a new future where individuals and groups would understand that the subtle field of energy we live in (and continuously entrain with) is as important as the physical attributes of our lives—or actually, even more important.

The quality of the energy in your environment is impacting you at every moment. To be uplifted today and for years to come, it's important to fill your environment with positive vibrational energy waves. We're distracted at increasing speeds—through rampant EMFs, damage to the environment, the quality of our food and air, and the conditioning of our thoughts by media and advertising. My time with Tony and Sage Robbins affirmed that one of the greatest performers in the self-development field was now consciously altering his energetic environment so that he would maintain the highest state. I knew others would soon follow.

Thank you for joining me as a pioneer in this movement to be a conscious co-creator of your space, for an enhanced physical, mental, and spiritual state for yourself and those who enter it.

Moving off the Autism Spectrum

While I was grateful to be given the opportunity to serve Tony and Sage Robbins and the Tony Robbins Foundation, my second story proved to be even more illuminating about the impact of the quantum field.

Sue, a Canadian trauma therapist, had owned a Quantum Sound Miracle iQube for two years. An opportunity to move back to Canada arose and she returned to her home, where her sister and nephew had been living. Her sister had a fifteen-year-old son who had been diagnosed as being on the autism spectrum and was only able to attend school in special classes. After around eighteen months cohabiting with her sister and nephew, with her Miracle iQube running its healing frequencies daily, Sue felt intuitively that there might have been some significant shifts in her nephew's abilities and performance. It had been three years since his initial test. Sue requested that her nephew's school retest his classroom placement. While the school personnel were adamant that there was likely to be no change, they agreed to redo the test. Much to their surprise, Sue's nephew's test results had radically transformed. He was now able to be placed in all normal classrooms. The school was flummoxed. They had never seen this happen before and they wanted to know what on earth had changed.

To me, this uplifting story makes sense, but to a school that is unfamiliar with entrainment and upwiring in such an extraordinary way, this felt like they had time-traveled to the future. A child has a receptive mind, and entrainment is faster due to the enhanced neuroplasticity factor. By resonating alongside quantum sound technology and stimulating his frontal lobe, a rebalancing of cognitive function and a stabilization of emotions occurred. Exposure to quantum technologies supported a rapid-fire transformation to break the boxes he had been pigeonholed into.

He was breaking the habit of being himself! This child, of course, did not have any knowledge of the field he was living in, alongside the Miracle. And, to be honest, neither did his mother. The transformation occurred without expectations of any kind.

Pain Reduction

I'll leave you with one final story of a miracle. An excellent energy and massage therapist in Southern California, Kerri Finnecy, was applying the Quantum Sound Miracle in her practice, alongside Voice Code therapy (see chapter 5). One of Kerri's clients, Jan, became fascinated and decided to invest in a Quantum Sound Miracle.

Jan's significant other had been injured in a serious motorcycle accident and was in continual pain. After the prescriptions for painkillers had run out, he took to drinking beer. Despite the residual pain from his accident, he was a business owner and needed to remain functional to manage his company. At the end of each working day, though, he would numb the pain, drinking close to twenty beers every night.

We advised Jan not to make a big deal about the Quantum Sound Miracle. Just let it be. She took the Quantum Sound

Miracle into her home without any drama or explanation. She just allowed it to play. She had no expectations. A couple of months after she began running the machine, we received the news that her husband had stopped drinking excessively. Without any conscious decision to end his addiction to alcohol, his altered resonance from the quantum technology naturally shifted him to a state where a social beer was a treat but the compulsion to drink his pain into oblivion was gone. This is a clear indication that somehow the pain decreased, or his pain threshold increased, due to increased production of endorphins and serotonin.

Once again, the designer field of the technology had done the heavy lifting by shifting this man's mental and physical state.

This universal quantum intelligence informs the field and everything in it. Through positive information provided to your cells, your brain, and your consciousness, an upgrade occurs to one of unlimited potential. Your food is upgraded, the pets in your home are calmer, your plants are more nourished! Across every aspect of your life, an uplift in vibration manifests at a physical and subconscious level.

Mind-blowing, isn't it? That waves of pure energy, sound, and light can infinitely improve your life! My point in sharing these stories is that this quantum field can be designed to support your highest quantum potential and to improve your clients through the healing process. Through tapping into the universal intelligence of quantum theory and entrainment, a portal opens for enhanced wellness and neuroplasticity benefits. It's a transformation that is science based, and yet the results are often perceived as miracles.

CHAPTER 5

Hack 2:
Voice Code Analysis

What's in Your Voice Is in Your Life

Did you know that every single human voice on planet earth is unique? Like the human thumbprint, the frequencies of your voice are unique. Isn't it mind-boggling to consider there isn't a single person on the planet who has the exact same blend of frequencies to communicate wants and needs to others that you do? Contemplate this for a moment.

Does it inspire you when you realize your voice is your unique signature and it reveals your blueprint? It inspires me. What is truly magnificent about this is that the human voice is so easily measurable. Therefore, I call it the Voice Code. Your Voice Code is unique to you, and it can be easily and quickly measured through a complex algorithm.

It is my intention to reveal to you how to efficiently address the underlying "subterranean" subconscious blocks that are impacting your life and your clients' lives, and to create a quantum dynamic field in your life that both automatically releases your subconscious blocks and heals you and your clients 24-7.

This culmination of forty years of research, technological development, and experimentation in the field causes an end to the repetitive "downwiring" triggered continually by events in the external world.

The audio track generated by your voice becomes a tuning fork that can automatically and continuously adjust and massage your energy field, rebalance old trauma, harmonize your stress, and release your deepest fears. It is the groundwork for every healing modality on the planet. It is through repetitive listening that the soundtrack vibrates away or loosens the patterns held in the subconscious.

We can consider the human voice as reflecting a mixture of our DNA combined with the emotional journey we have embarked on. It is a doorway to our subconscious and can reveal our deep inner workings, emotions, feelings, and beliefs.

Your vibration is completely unique, and it is measurable.

It's not just the shape and size of your vocal cords that make your voice exclusively yours, but your emotions, your history, your memories, and your psychological state. In many ways, I like to consider each person's voice as an entry point to their Akashic records.

In this very moment, your voice is not only reflecting the balance of your chakras, but it may well indicate your future decisions, hopes, and dreams.

The Psychic Drill

Due to these facts, the quickest route to reach your subconscious congestions is through the unique blend of frequencies revealed when your voice is assessed. Your voice will quickly reveal the terrain you have traveled and the path you are about to embark on. The voice is the easiest way to access the vibration of an individual.

I like to describe our Voice Code Analysis process as being like a psychic drill. Our algorithm picks up on your frequency dams and creates a new vibration as a soundtrack that can bust your energy congestion with precisely formulated frequencies that vibrate through the dam wall to spew the muck right out of you. It's a welcome release when you sense the vibrations creating relief. I liken this quantum sound healing work to a shortcut back to someone's authentic self, a self that is then freed from the quagmire of the daily grind.

The ability to access this in seconds is truly a hack.

The Blind Spot in Our Story

When I worked in the clinics and hospitals of some of the great avatars and saints of India, this inability to work on the subconscious realm was revealed quite dramatically. Even when I was in front of great saints and spiritual seekers, I would recognize their dysfunctional relationships with their significant others and children. Although an individual would be pursuing a life of conscious evolution and spiritual growth, and essentially working on themselves full time, there were gaps that were often reflected in their relationships and family life.

My unique gift is that I was able to see these gaps—the holes within the soul—that remained damaged. It was painful to see these subconscious memories lurking behind the scenes, waiting to erupt.

So, what I was seeing on the outside as a person approached the *darshan* of a holy saint was not what was going on in their actual lives. There was a huge gap—a blind spot.

This is a reality I have found to be true for so many people who are addicted to a path of self-help, transformation, and spirituality. No matter the Zen moments grasped in meditation, retreats, or in the presence of gurus, some part remains unhealed. It is never hidden for very long, revealing itself from the subconscious as an eruption when something triggers stress.

I was fortunate in that when I asked the universe for a tool, a technique, a modality that would yield efficient results in my talk therapy, hypnotherapy, and past-life-regression practice, I was eventually guided to Voice Analysis. It became the underpinning of all that I would do for the rest of this incarnation.

I didn't only train as a psychotherapist (at the University of Chicago); I was also qualified in hypnotherapy (my doctoral thesis was in hypnosis), rebirthing, Reiki, massage, moral development, and psychic surgery, to name but a few. I was often trained and mentored by the best of the best in their field. But it was the Voice Analysis that provided the supplementary soundtrack to improve all results, no matter who I had received my qualifications from. Voice Analysis addresses the blind spot in each of us. It was the support structure for me that would reveal and address the subconscious blocks that most can't see. As I worked with the other modalities I had been trained in, I utilized Voice Analysis to create improved results in my clients, using the soundtrack that the software generated with the file created by Robert Lloy.

We can't see or know how the subconscious is operating to control our lives. Aha! This is the beauty—the voice reveals all of this. The audio track generated by an analysis of billions of bits of vocal information would release this energetically as I performed in my licensed modality.

Why is this, you might ask.

The design of Voice Code Analysis and the frequencies it generates is purposefully crafted to address these subconscious issues. The inability to mask your inner truth—even from yourself—is like opening up your soul, but in an objective, neutral, scientific way.

You cannot hide or mask the frequencies in your voice—even from yourself. It is like lying naked and revealing your soul to someone in an objective, neutral way. Nothing is hidden. Every other therapy and process involves some interpretation, through which something can be projected, distorted, or hidden from the observer, client, or practitioner.

In quantum physics, it is an established fact that the observer can alter what is being observed. So, this would imply that the healer, just by observing someone's state, can alter the particles and the cells around them. When you consider quantum physics alongside healing modalities, it becomes even more evident how important it is to ensure the frequencies supporting your work are devoid of the clutter and stress you may be carrying, especially regarding energetic burnout.

Dr. Emoto's Prophecy on Sound Therapy

Dr. Masaru Emoto wrote about our Voice Code work in his book *The True Power of Water: Healing and Discovering Ourselves*.

> *If this new system becomes popular, sound therapy would be able to make a quantum leap, because the sound with the most suitable information can be delivered to our*

individual cells.... Mr. Lloy developed software capable of creating a suitable sound after having a person vocalize for fifteen seconds.... I tried it myself. As I was exhausted after overseas travel and I was also quite busy writing, I had very stiff shoulders and some pain. After listening to the sound created by the software for thirty minutes, the stiffness in my shoulders suddenly disappeared (page 124).

By complementing your work with sound, you take the heavy lifting out of it. It ends up not only creating better results for your clients, but you as the facilitator of transformation become more balanced and powerful within your domain.

Consider yourself for just a moment as a fluid quantum being of infinite potential. Then there are a bunch of frozen blocks in the fluidity. They are rigid aspects of you that block your flow of greatness. You can't talk these blocks away, because they are stuck patterns of energy. Frequency can address these frozen blocks by massaging them and addressing them repeatedly. A Voice Code is like a magical massage that addresses these frozen blocks of energy repeatedly.

This is the beauty of the customized audio track that is generated by the analysis of your voice. You can listen to it repeatedly until the frozen blocks of energy, which we may call your beliefs or personality, are released and dissolved. I recommend listening to this once or twice a day.

You won't need to become a therapist with years of insight into how these blocks were created. You won't need to become a master intuitive or a medical intuitive. The voice will automatically reveal what your clients have repressed. The audio soundtrack that is provided will then act as an intuitive, psychic drill to release and melt these patterns away. The soundtrack will automatically address what is lurking within the subconscious and creating obstacles in the path of desire.

The Voice Code has the potential to show us what chakras are in and out of balance and to reveal the deepest subconscious stresses and fears on an energetic level.

Your voice also gives us a very clear diagnostic tool that reveals instantly the frequencies that will attune and align you with a greater sense of harmony, peace, and well-being. Makes sense, doesn't it?

Frequency in Motion

You are frequency in motion, ever changing and adapting to your environment. Herein lies the problem. You are always evolving with what's around you, mirroring it and resonating with it. This principle is called *resonance*. So, if your emotions are out of balance, this will be reflected almost instantly in your chakras and your energy field, and therefore in your voice. Think of it like a poker player's tell.

The voice provides us with a map of the entire energetic structure of every human being, regardless of age, sex, caste, or sexual preference. Think of the soothing voice of a radio announcer compared with the unhappy voice of a person sick in hospital. Imbalances can also be revealed through the frequency of the whinny of a horse, the bark of a dog, or the meow of a cat, or, for that matter, through the voice of any animal that emits sound.

Wouldn't this indicate that the voice is the preferred energetic measurement tool for all therapies? The foundation, the essence? It cannot lie. You cannot cover, mask, or distort the frequencies. They are simply there when you speak or utter any sound. It is impossible to repress or disguise the blend of frequencies in the voice.

Whether it's a baby's cry or an adult's shriek, the voice can, in only fifteen seconds, provide us with a map of an individual's entire energetic structure. Every time that person vocalizes, their unique blend of frequencies broadcasts their physical, emotional, mental, and spiritual states of being. It's incredible, right?

Noted sound healer Kay Gardner says in her book *Sounding the Inner Landscape: Music as Medicine,* "The human voice conveys who you are through a unique combination of rhythm, melody, timbre, and dynamics. It not only reveals who you are, but it also reveals from what sphere you draw your greatest energy."

The core physical and emotional issues of every human being on the planet are reflected in what is being expressed through their voice. Robert Lloy says, "The human voice is the repository of the emotional body." The state of balance or imbalance, the health or disease of the organs, the core psychological or emotional patterns, and the lifelong habits of both strengths and weaknesses are reflected in voice emissions.

Are you following me still on the significance of this information? Your voice can reveal every facet of you; it is the doorway to your subconscious mind. The work by me and Robert Lloy on voice analysis, known as Voice Code Analysis, is the area where we have garnered the most recognition. With mathematical simplicity, your unique vocal resonance taps into your subconscious blockages—issues, stories, energy stagnations, and more—that have been dominating you throughout your entire time on this planet. Therefore, the simplicity and speed of access of Voice Code Analysis provides the perfect complementary tool to any and all alternative or energetic modalities.

For a free "Find Your Frequency" consult with me, go to calendly.com/quantumsoundtherapy.

You may wonder how the Voice Code Analysis is accomplished. Let me try to explain.

There are three stages.

Stage One: Analysis of the Human Voice

With our voice we are broadcasting a vibration that is essentially a blend of sound frequencies, a vocal structure that can be mapped and analyzed with incredible precision to reveal character strengths and weaknesses. As it is impossible to repress or disguise our individual frequencies, the voice becomes the most reliable window into human consciousness, reflecting our issues clearly and precisely—and providing a route to self-healing through sound. While we cannot truly override the subconscious mind, we can release the traumatic wounds and resolve the unhealed pains it holds.

The secret lies in the five octave frequencies of the human voice. The subterranean subconscious is hidden within these frequencies and running the show. Our Voice Code Analysis, developed over forty years, analyzes over one billion bits of information from the human voice over a span of five octaves, using the refined algorithm developed by Robert Lloy.

By analyzing the range of the five octaves and pinpointing the subconscious, we get a deep insight into the client's vocal frequencies.

Voice Code Analysis will detect what is hidden in the frequencies; it is the key to cracking open the safe, revealing the long-ago secrets, unspoken beliefs, and unwelcome-yet-stored memories and emotions that have kept you from reaching your unlimited potential. This is the terrain where you must tread if you are to truly manifest the dictates of, for example, the laws of attraction, visualization, and affirmations.

Stage Two: Creating a Harmonizing Soundtrack

Entering your energy field through the doorway of your voice allows us to peer into the contents of your subconscious on a frequency level. Through the accurate analysis of the millions of frequencies in the human voice, the dissonance is identified and corrected. The development of a customized audio track is stage two.

Stage Three: Using the Created Voice Code

The vibrations and sound waves within these five octaves can then be manipulated via a harmonizing soundtrack to transform the client while they are working, relaxing, playing, meditating, or sleeping. By sending the balanced frequencies back to vibrate someone's essence, the hold of their various subconscious patterns is lessened in short order. The customized soundtrack vibrates away at the traumas so that they have less power and hold on you. I like to call this the "loosening effect." The sounds act to loosen the hold of the traumas, eventually dissolving these completely so that you are free to let go of the memory that has its hold on you.

This unique personalized soundtrack will, in minutes, balance, harmonize, and release the deepest subconscious blocks, determining the balancing frequencies that will release the pent-up energies like a psychic drill. It very gently uproots and vibrationally releases memories from the subconscious. Therefore, some people, after just a few sessions, are able to suddenly let go of lifelong limitations, blocks, and belief systems. Most people report feeling freer, lighter, as though a load has been lifted from them, even after one or two sessions.

The client usually becomes aware almost immediately of what is being released, because the issue usually erupts into their consciousness and introduces itself to them as an emotion they have been repressing, one that is quite familiar in their story.

Therefore, it makes perfect sense that by adding Voice Analysis to any modality, we would enhance our results as healers, therapists, energy practitioners, body workers, and coaches.

The beauty of this is that you can accelerate the process of any treatment—whether it is emotional, mental, psychological, or physical—simply by administering an audio track of sound frequencies precisely tailored to the individual's voice code.

If you don't do this for yourself and your client, you risk continuing the client's emotional roller-coaster ride of ups and downs. You may sink into overwhelm and burnout. As we know, this process of transformation can become like a broken record, with patterns repeating over and over again. Also, you may miss the window to process this material so you can elevate yourself and thrive in a new, coherent frequency of clarity, love, and sound, and do the same for your client.

Pinpointing subconscious blocks and mastering neuro-plasticity at a frequency level uproots issues and releases them. Frequency is the key to transforming your life and your clients' results. Not only that, my hacks are efficient, easy to understand, and require very little training. Consider this book and my lifelong lessons the solutions you have been seeking to up-level all areas of your life.

Voice Code Analysis Reveals the Hidden Blueprint in the Subconscious

I have been using the Voice Analysis process as a supportive modality in the transformation process for my private psychotherapy practice since I had that Upper West Side Manhattan office. Even then, I knew I was searching for the tool to depict and release the subconscious without thousands of hours of talk psychotherapy. Even as a teen, I was keen to distance myself from the Band-Aid effect of most therapies. I knew there was a solution beyond providing comfort and a safe cocoon for trauma.

Intuitively, I sensed that underneath the realm of consciousness, the subconscious was running the show. All those hours interning only demonstrated that the modalities I was studying were not capable of accurately reaching deep into the subconscious realm. I could see and sense that part of the client before me was always stuck and unhealed.

Five Octaves Release the "Memory" of Your Story

Over time with my practice, I noticed that as I generated customized audio tracks for my clients and released their compromised or weakened frequencies, their lifelong energetic blueprint began to shift and repattern spontaneously. Do you remember those old-school kaleidoscopes? Each round with the Voice Analysis software was like a rotation of the kaleidoscope, with the client's "picture" evolving into an ever-more beautiful state. I didn't need the same focus on interventions or talk therapy. Their patterns—the way they related to their partners and children, their work, diet, physicality, and efforts with exercise—began to shift toward their true self and a life of purpose, intuition, and passion. These shifted before my eyes. Lifelong structural personality, emotional patterns, and behavioral patterns, such as codependency, fear, insomnia, and even addictions, would shift and transform—sometimes overnight.

It was during my time implementing Voice Analysis alongside my more traditional modalities that I began to understand how the subconscious controlled most of our behavior. And that each of those predominant components was a secret hidden in plain sight. It's much like a dream where you find yourself naked in a classroom—only this is far more socially acceptable—with your exposed, individualized voice patterns being laid bare. It is just there, hidden in the five octaves.

Releasing Unconscious Influences

In the early stages of my relationship to the voice as a gateway to unconscious influences, beliefs, and decision making, I thought it possible to address the subconscious through the voice. After decades of experience and exposure to staggering results, I unlocked the secret: the voice reveals all, offering the fastest hack to our most repressed memories, in our energy field.

I've witnessed healing modalities significantly amplify their results because of their attention to addressing the subconscious. Through attending to deep-rooted problems, the modality—whether it's Reiki, massage, therapy, or something else—is ten times more successful, and positive change is evident in the client. As a healer-coach, you know the result of a fulfilled client on an energetic level—it's almost impossible to keep positive results a secret when your client is radiating their upgraded vibrations. As my mentor and co-creator Robert Lloy says, "What's in your voice is in your life."

Transformation Story 1:
Frustrated Wife Doris

I'm going to share some stories of how the Voice Analysis and the audio track it generates created quantum shifts in a few of the people I have worked with.

My client Doris offers the perfect anecdote to illustrate this point. A professional woman in her forties, Doris had been married seven times. Every time she got fed up, angry, or upset at her then-husband, she would walk out. And then promptly find another one. It was a classic case of fight, flight, or freeze. With Doris the impulse was always to run—fast.

Doris wanted to address this, and for years had been trialing therapies, treatments, and self-improvement techniques to alleviate her destructive behavior in her intimate relationships. Nothing penetrated those subconscious blocks, and at the end of her tether with husband seven, she found me.

It was clear that Voice Analysis was the laser-efficient modality that would penetrate Doris's long-buried patterns. I like to consider these deeply buried subconscious patterns as frozen blocks encoded in the energy system; they effortlessly unravel when the correct frequencies are applied repetitively. The frequencies "melt" these frozen blocks that are like icebergs in the defense structure of the personality. These frozen icebergs can prevent people from manifesting the life of their dreams or the law of attraction. When these begin to melt, the horizon becomes brighter, more unlimited and expansive. My clients usually relate to this immediately by reporting a sensation of lightness. "I feel so much lighter, freer, more expanded."

Another block in the history of human consciousness is dissolved into frequency and quantum energy. I always feel that this baby step is a huge step in the evolution of humanity, as it can result in the trajectory of a person's life being permanently altered.

While I ran the Voice Code Analysis during several of Doris's sessions, it was on session two that she had her first *aha* moment. She felt agitated after our hour together, and as she was cooking dinner, husband number seven said something irritating to her.

For about thirty minutes, Doris slammed the kitchen cabinet doors and created some havoc in the environment to outwardly express her irritation. She was experiencing the feeling that usually kicked off her flight mode (and her search for her next husband), only this time she was able to identify that pattern for what it was. Doris was now experiencing a deep energetic release of the anger she had been repressing for many years. The energy of the sound frequencies she had received had facilitated the release of the deep-seated tension and anger that was at the core of the defense structure of this pattern.

After this dramatic release of the initial tension, Doris's work was not quite done. She continued to listen to her audio track and have further sessions until she could identify, at a deep cellular level, that her repressed anger had been released by the sound. During the ten sessions with me that complemented this release, we worked through a reprogramming and rebalancing of her old habits so that she didn't feel the urge to run every time her husband triggered anger.

This is precisely why the customized audio track based on the frequencies of a client's voice can support and enhance all energetic modalities. It can reach more deeply into the subconscious, where the underlying memories, traumas, and pains are stored.

The pulsation of the sound breaks up the stasis, the rigidity of the ego, and the identity structure where the trauma and the defenses are so strong. The sound can bypass the person's armor and resistance. The more subtle it is, the more powerful it is, because we don't know how to resist it. The sound frequencies are working directly on the old armor formed in the brain, and they create a metamorphosis at a structural and energetic level.

If everything has a sound component, then integrating sound into your healer-coach practice can only enhance your results. It's like adding feng shui to your already beautiful home. It adds the invisible component that continues to work, dissolving the hardened, frozen ego structure that has become such an impediment to living. Adding this invisible sound design realigns the ego structure constantly so that your results as a healer are amplified, multiplied, and accelerated.

Transformation Story 2:
Divorcée Tiffany

Encountering a client whom I'll call Tiffany, I found out that she had experienced her second marital separation. It had occurred suddenly after an intense argument, and she had abruptly filed for divorce.

I had worked previously with Tiffany therapeutically in an ashram setting in India, when she experienced her first traumatic separation and subsequent divorce. While she was falling in love, settling into a new relationship, and then moving on from it, I too was moving on, with my Voice Code Analysis work.

I explained to Tiffany that I was working with this breakthrough modality that employed sound frequencies to pinpoint underlying issues. Instead of a lengthy talk session diving deeply into the argument and her relationship history, I would run my Voice Analysis technology for two minutes, and then, after playing the customized recording in my office, she would be free to replay it at home.

As an aside, the therapy in the office is supplemented with an audio-track chip that the client can bring home. It's like a client taking their energy healer home with them. They can have as many sessions as they want, listening to the customized audio track. If something throws them off balance, they have the tuning-fork audio track in their pocket, so to speak. Just the thought of having this "gift" from the healer adds tremendous value to your session. It is a comfort and a support. As well, it can anchor the client in a positive, high-vibrational state.

Following the tumultuous argument and separation, Tiffany was back to raising her three children as a single parent.

I was confident that the voice analysis would assist in dealing with the emotional pain and upheaval she was experiencing.

Tiffany's relief in that first playing of her voice analysis was immediate. She later commented on the release she felt when the emotional weight from the premature termination of her marriage lifted: "I felt lighter and happier than I have after any therapy session, like a burden had been lifted. And it lasted much longer than any other therapy session. The sound frequencies removed deep levels of pain and fear!"

Tiffany and I continued to explore and release Tiffany's blockages, using the frequencies to stabilize her emotionally. As Tiffany's lifelong fears and anxieties around loneliness and abandonment surfaced, she was on an emotional roller coaster.

However, as Tiffany was preparing to finalize her divorce, her husband reappeared with an entirely new outlook on their marriage. He was resonating in the field of Tiffany's clarity and love, and this shifted his perspective on her and their marriage. A new vibration of coherence and harmony entered their relationship. Because Tiffany had worked on her issues and developed a heightened level of self-love, the couple were able to recommence their romance on entirely new terms. Tiffany was able to express what she desired in their relationship and, most importantly, receive it. As I write this, Tiffany and her husband have restructured their life and recently moved to Florida to pursue their dreams.

Tiffany opened the gateway to greater self-love and fulfillment the moment she committed to her process of self-healing through sound. By penetrating the defense structure at a subconscious level, the sound frequencies opened new gateways for personality and behavior shifts toward her soul's true expression. Without repressive thought, self-denial, and self-hatred, Tiffany was free from those former shackles.

The customized frequencies chip away at the ego's defenses and the subconscious. As it is a soundtrack, it is portable and can be used even on your iPhone, any time of the day or night, when you need a tune-up.

This lightens the load for everyone. We are simply restructuring and harmonizing the vibratory pattern, balancing the chakras, and giving the subtle energy field exactly what it needs to thrive. Does it get any better than that?

From Chakra Misalignment
to Chakra Alignment

Prior to listening to their personalized voice code, a person's chakras are misaligned. After listening to their voice code, a person's chakras align themselves.

To try this for yourself, go to quantumsoundtherapy.com/cloud-sound-therapy for a 50-percent discount coupon on our Cloud Sound Therapy Single Session and enter the code GETMYFREQUENCIESNOW1.

And for a free "Find Your Frequency" consult with me, go to quantumsoundtherapy.com/cloud-sound-therapy.

CHAPTER 6

Hack 3:
Unleashing Your Genius

The Unlimited Potential of the
Left Frontal Lobe

Smarter comes first because everything else is easier when your brain reaches peak performance. Just a decade ago, most people believed that you couldn't actually get smarter.

Dave Asprey, *Game Changers*

Neuroscientists, researchers, and personal development gurus call the brain's left frontal lobe "the seat of genius." Exploring the potential of this realm is like opening a gateway to quantum potential that is both unlimited and inspired. Conscious frequency-based activation of the left frontal lobe is the secret key that allows us to make decisions and choices different from those we may have made in the past. Therefore, it is the key that holds the power of your transformation and the transformation of your clients. Activating the left frontal lobe during an emotional crisis will result in an entirely out-of-the-box outcome. In many ways, it is the key to becoming more resourceful and to generating more success in your work and more flow in your finances.

What would happen if we taught our children to focus on the brainwave state they are in and on the part of the brain that is dominant at that particular moment? It is simple. We would live in a more conscious reality, where people would be managing their consciousness instead of being trapped by it.

We each possess the capability to transform the repetitive behaviors that no longer serve us. The innate capacity for change that is hidden within our physiology is extraordinary. When we can tap into that capability, it is like finding the high-power switch on a hair dryer: it's full blast—all systems are liberating your quantum potential. When you comprehend not only the possibility but also how to get there yourself, a switch flicks on, and a life of unlimited possibilities unfolds.

A Single Test Score

The story that I am about to tell is the unfolding of one young man's potential for transformation. It illustrates the pure quantum potential that is in all of us if we can awaken to the opportunity. The frontal lobe is the gateway to an enhanced result. By switching on the frontal lobe, we can stop allowing our amygdala to run the show. The amygdala is a small area in the limbic system, the primitive brain that was wired to survive the harsh environment humans lived in thousands of years ago.

This tale is one close to my heart. It is the story of my son, Mike Reilly. While this is one story in hundreds from our tribe, it illustrates a dramatic change in a young man's life through brain upwiring during his studies for the Graduate Management Admission Test (GMAT), the standardized test used in the US for entrance to graduate schools in finance and business.

While I do not agree with the weight of a single test score, whether it's the SAT, the GMAT, or whatever other test your children have to go through, I recognize it is still a reality that to achieve the goal of college admission, necessary for many careers, these tests are part of the path that has to be followed. Mike's dream was to be an investment banker, and a score of 700 or above on the GMAT was a crucial step toward that dream.

Mike's story is not about improving a test score. Instead, it's about upwiring or rewiring his brain. It demonstrates the extreme capabilities that, through neuroplasticity, can change a person's outlook, their feeling about themselves, and the trajectory of their life. By understanding and using brain hacks, we can change our life in unfathomable ways; in children's or young adults' brains, those changes are often faster and more dramatic.

All this, and we didn't even believe in neuroplasticity until about ten years ago. Crazy, huh?

"If I'm Not Smart Enough"

August 1, 2010: the phone rings. My son Mike is calling me in frustration. He has just completed his sophomore year at the State University of New York College in Cortland. Having taken three years to play junior hockey at the pro level, he was twenty-three at the time. When I picked up my phone, I heard

Mike say, "I keep getting a 500 or 550 on my practice GMAT. **If I'm not smart enough** to get an MBA, I've decided it is okay with me."

These are the wrong words to say to a therapist mom who has devoted her life to helping people fulfill their dreams (whatever they may be) and find their unique genius and purpose.

The upwiring thinking would look something like this: "I'm not performing well on these GMAT tests. How do I change this?"

Many young adults are stopped at the entrance gates to elite business programs by this single number alone. Mike had begun studying for the GMAT the summer after his freshman year of college. This was one month before he actually took the test in August. He also had set aside the summer of his sophomore year to prepare for the GMAT while doing an internship in finance. He was not alone in requiring this much time to study for such a complex business-standards test.

When I heard Mike express those powerful words, "not smart enough," I was surprised, but also shocked and disappointed. As his mom and with my background, I was aware of the impact of the subconscious and of unconscious thought on our outcomes, and I had thought my son understood that too. Mike had always been a go-getter, with a brilliant, inquisitive mind, and he was always ready to tackle the next challenge. Since he had been a child, people had always commented on his innate intelligence and problem-solving ability, even with his extracurricular performance in hockey.

Was it possible that one test score could destroy his confidence and self-worth? And with it, his career? I was confused about where his self-doubt was coming from. What was the root of his issue with this test? Where were the lack of integration and his limiting beliefs stemming from? As a parent, I was concerned about the impact this would have on Mike's future.

I felt an urgency to act. I had to uncover the key to unlock this issue from his subconscious and do all that I could to ensure his destiny wouldn't be impacted by a trapped, unconscious misbelief.

Little did I know that the key to Mike's performance (and everyone's performance, for that matter) lay in a little-understood area of the brain known as the frontal lobe.

A Customized Soundtrack from Mike's Five Octaves

Remember the amygdala's emergency response of fight, flight, or freeze? In full mother mode, of course, I launched into action. I was ready to do all that I could to fight for my son's goals, as long as he was willing. I told Mike we would create a special soundtrack that would target his left frontal lobe to help him study. We made plans for him to come home on Tuesday, August 17, to study for seven days for the GMAT, and then scheduled an appointment for him to take the actual GMAT nearby on August 25.

My partner Robert Lloy (the creator of Scalar Wave technology) and I were ready for action. I knew we needed a special soundtrack for the frontal lobe that would target Mike's ability to focus. It would need to accelerate learning and activate the genius that I knew my son (and your children too) had access to. One week before Mike arrived home, we started creating a soundtrack to help him score really well on his test. That gave him one final week of study before his GMAT. It was crunch time.

I was profoundly inspired by Mike's challenge. I understand the significance of this cry for help. It is the cry of so many who have had their hopes and dreams crushed by a simple test, a number on a page that either qualifies them or bars them from their goal. In South Korea, mothers will write on many prayer sticks and hold prayer events to help their children attain the desired number on an SAT, GMAT, or LSAT, knowing it is the gateway, the price of entrance to a better destiny.

While of course my driving force was to do all that I could to support my son, I also understood the implications for children and adults throughout the world if we could get this soundtrack right. This was an opportunity to increase the brain's power, performance, and creativity in young and old alike. A focus-specific sound program had been on my mind for some time, but I had postponed it in favor of other priorities. My son's dilemma shifted it from the vision board to reality in record time.

Our target was to activate Mike's frontal lobe to allow him to focus for longer periods of time. Using the Quantum Sound Miracle iQube, the soundtrack would run the correct frequencies to achieve this, and it would run 24-7 while he was home for his intense period of study. These new sound frequencies would stimulate the subtle energy of his frontal lobe, working on the principles of sound entrainment and energetic shifts. In theory, Mike's learning would accelerate and his comprehension of the material would strengthen. So that we could serve our tribe better in the future, we wanted to measure this new software. Using Mike's GMAT test scores as the benchmarks, we would be able to see the improvement between the practice test and the real one. We also monitored the length of time Mike was able to study intensely, as well as his emotional reactions. Would he be discouraged and frustrated as he studied, ready to throw in the towel on his dream career?

Could we upwire and rewire Mike's brain in seven days for improved test scores? Could we get him from his 500-plus scores to the 700-or-above mark? The 700 mark is what would allow him entrance into the more elite finance and business schools he wanted to attend. If you're a parent, you know the worry that your child will not fulfill the potential you can see in them. What if Mike's confidence was so impaired that he quit? Could we help Mike be smarter and faster and accelerate his learning? I knew I had to try.

Mike was receptive to the offer of a customized frontal lobe soundtrack—so much so that he was both nervous and excited about the seven days of study ahead. We set Mike up in our study with the Quantum Sound Miracle iQube next to his desk, and he got to work.

On the first day of study, Mike took another practice test and scored around 550 again. He continued to study continuously for three days, taking breaks only for meals and light workouts. All the while, the designated frequencies were emanating from the iQube, calming him and enhancing his ability to concentrate. So much was on the line here, and I felt his anxiety and concern building while his future hung in the balance.

On day four, Mike took another practice test. The real test was then only three days away, and we all felt the stress building. It was a beautiful summer's evening, and I sat poolside while Mike was inside taking the test. I heard shouting from inside the house and ran to discover Mike jumping for joy—he had gotten 690 on the practice test! Wow!

Mike had broken his barrier and expanded his quantum potential. Euphoria was mixed with relief. Thanks to the focus soundtrack, his brain was smarter and faster—upwired. As a parent, most importantly, I felt elation that Mike had exceeded his belief of what he could attain in a few short days.

The change in Mike's test score indicated that our experimental soundtrack had worked to switch on Mike's frontal lobe so he could more fully integrate and apply what he was studying.

But would this change endure the stress of the actual testing environment, where he would have to perform without the soundtrack and the iQube? Or would performance anxiety kick in and downwire his brain?

Two Official Test Scores

On the drive to the test center, I found I was far more nervous than Mike. Over the three days that had followed that 690 score, Mike had continued to learn, focus, concentrate, and review. We even had the soundtrack running through the iQube in the car. Due to the intensity of the upwiring, Mike had zero anxiety—the true sign that he was in his frontal cortex. And there was I in the amygdala, in full mother mode. Mike went into the exam center confident and relaxed, and three hours later he emerged with an official test score of 640 on the real GMAT. He had fulfilled his goal and broken through the ceiling of his performance. He felt like a real winner.

On his return to college, we armed Mike with his own Quantum Sound iQube and the pre-loaded focus soundtrack. He left our nest with a complete one-eighty on his attitude and his outlook for the future. He intuitively understood that he had smashed his former limitations and that his capacity would only continue to expand. With a new mindset of "I am smart enough," Mike's whole world transformed. That level of optimism and unlimited potential is contagious.

As a result of this uplift in his capabilities, he studied more, received a 4.1 average, was elected to the honor society, and graduated summa cum laude. He was also awarded the Chairs Award for Academic Excellence in Economics. We had managed to use our technology not only to switch Mike's frontal lobe on but to keep it running on full power. The neuroplasticity of someone at the age of twenty-three is unlimited.

Mike's mission to get into a graduate school for finance was not over. He returned to college to prepare for a second GMAT test. He needed a 700 or above to be admitted to his goal program—the Vanderbilt Master of Science in Finance, a program that only admits thirty students per year worldwide.

The Quantum Sound iQube ran beside his desk during his study sessions, and his frontal lobe continued to fire. He exuded confidence in his abilities, which placed him on the Vanderbilt University waitlist. They had told him at his interview that the only thing holding him back was his GMAT score.

On February 7, 2012, I received a phone call from Mike. "I did it! I got a 710. I couldn't have done this without you, Mom, or the focus soundtrack!"

Cue proud Mom moment.

Mike was accepted at Vanderbilt University with twenty-nine other bright sparks.

What struck me, as Mike's mother, throughout this period was how fulfilling it was to see his frontal lobe switched on and to witness his transformation.

To see your child become more at peace with himself is one of the most fulfilling moments in life. At times, I would remark that it felt I had another son. He was operating in the zone of his true quantum potential—at a level that he had not been able to envision in the past.

Your Brain's Most Valuable Real Estate: The Frontal Lobe

The frontal lobe makes choices that support our desire for a particular outcome. When we use this part of our brain to its capacity, our behavior matches our purpose, and our actions match our intent—our mind and body are one. How many times have our behavior and purpose matched completely?

Joe Dispenza,
Breaking the Habit of Being Yourself

My son's story clearly demonstrates that when one has the will, the intent, and the tools, maximum levels of neuroplasticity are possible, seeming miracles occur, and life changes result. Mike became the master of his destiny.

Neuroplasticity is the word that best describes the brain's innate capacity to make these new connections and create new opportunities and accomplishments from these connections.

The technology of the Quantum Sound iQubes applies five key activation principles that are essential to enhanced mastery and success. I will be revealing these soon.

Through conscious application of these five activation principles, you will amplify and accelerate your results in all endeavors, across all areas of your life. If you're like I was with Mike, you are prepared to do whatever it takes to turn on the real estate in the frontal lobe that you're naturally endowed with. Mike's transformation was like finding him living in a downtown studio and then finding he'd upgraded to an oceanside mansion. Think about it. You have the opportunity to upgrade your mind to use your frontal lobe's fullest potential.

The frontal lobe holds the reins over the emotional self, where the amygdala and limbic system reside. It endows you with the capacity for conscious choice, free will, infinite creativity, and genius. Even if you don't believe this now, once that frontal lobe is activated, your quantum potential will be firing on all cylinders. It is that simple.

So how did it all turn out for Mike? He completed his master's degree in finance at Vanderbilt, and he beat over a thousand applicants to be offered a position as a financial analyst investment banker at a Fortune 500 company. Two years and two months after he started activating his frontal lobe, he had made a giant leap on the path to his destiny. He continues to thrive and is now working in private equity in his dream city of Denver.

I have moments of wondering how his life might have turned out without the tools that allowed him to reach his quantum potential.

While Mike's academic and career success makes me proud as a mother, his success is not the most important part of this story. From this activation, Mike has thrived and continues to strive for his goals. He has developed a practice of extreme neuroplasticity, and he will carry this throughout his life. The trajectory of Mike's life has evolved dramatically through this practice.

This quantum leap in Mike's evolution has revealed that most of us are capable of brilliantly accomplishing noble tasks if we simply dedicate ourselves to the evolution of our most precious real estate—the frontal lobe. Here lies the dormant genius and a set of gifts within each of us. Change comes from our simple willingness to switch on and intentionally evolve our innate capability through neuroplasticity.

In the movie *Groundhog Day*, Bill Murray's character victoriously changes the repetitive behavior that is keeping him stuck in the same day. Everyone has the same opportunity to adapt, to change, and to succeed—minus repeating the same day. We each have the potential to alter the brain's wired-together neurons, transform redundant habits, and attain liberation from self-imposed limitations. If you don't believe me, read Joe Dispenza's *Breaking the Habit of Being Yourself* (I refer to it a couple of times in chapter 4) and the list of references at the end of the book. By learning to use your brain in new ways, you can cultivate new neural pathways.

Version 2.0: The New You

With new frequencies, knowledge, or instruction, the consciousness becomes rewired, with heightened flexibility and adaptation to change. Extreme neuroplasticity, or upwiring, is the willingness to engage in new ideas, actions, and practices. Even reading this book is a wonderful exercise in neuroplasticity! Extreme neuroplasticity equals smarts, which equals enhanced results. Like exercise, neuroplasticity is enhanced by the Quantum Sound technology, and yet it is further amplified by exercises that require concentration, study, learning, focus, or movement. They act as companions to each other, complementing and enhancing the actual movements of energy in the brain.

As you'll have noticed in Mike's tale, change is cumulative and occurs daily when you consciously switch on your frontal lobe. Through the application of sound frequencies and the repetition of brain wave entrainment, along with intention, we can rewire ourselves and our children to create an enhanced future.

Are you ready to use your brain in a new way so that you can open the gateway to your genius and live your life from this space? You've got nothing to lose and everything to gain!

CHAPTER 7

Hack 4:
Awakening the Third Eye

W hat would change in your story if suddenly you could heighten your intuition and perceive your clients through your third eye? What would you see that you are not seeing now? What would you perceive? What actions would you take to accelerate positive results?

This is what all awakened healer-coaches can do to serve the planet at their highest level.

Consider this: if there is one thing all masters, teachers, and enlightened beings have in common, it is their opened third eye, which allows them to perceive and serve the universe, themselves, and the rest of us in a unique way.

Once one is awakened, from moment to moment the world changes. Maintaining this state in a world of density and pollution is the challenge.

There is a profound and fundamental shift in your consciousness. The contrast can be dramatic. You can suddenly see into people—their stories, their dramas, and their congested blocks of frozen energy—with incredible clarity.

If you are lucky, you may know exactly what to do with this information.

It's like the first time you realized your parents are human, not some kind of maternal and paternal demigods. Once you're conscious of their ability to err in the same way you do, your relationship to them changes.

So why is your awakened pineal gland significant to your development as a healer?

Simply stated, it makes your work and life easier and more fluid.

Look around your office or practice space. Is it lined with certifications, proudly hung to demonstrate your path of purpose and commitment to healing your community? These structured modalities and approaches give you the context and method to work within. They also give you confidence and knowledge. With the certificates and accolades, you receive a daily reminder that you're meant to be where you are, meant to be fast-tracking the awakened in your community to, in turn, lift the vibration of the masses.

However, there is another level you can perceive when you have access to your third-eye insights. When you are third-eye awakened, you see into the quantum field and the energy field of your client.

Plato Asks, "Will You Leave the Cave?"

This quantum hack is liberating. When you step over into this realm of operation, you will see things in an entirely new way, and the external world will no longer have the same hold on you. It is the freedom from bondage that Plato's cave allegory describes. Plato, the Greek philosopher, wrote about enlightenment. The question he posed was, when you "see the light" or become enlightened, do you leave the cave and share this state with others, or do you remain in the cave and keep this attainment to yourself?

I have had the pleasure of observing the awakening of many members of our tribe, along with the experience of my own awakening.

A couple of summers ago, I was teaching a pineal-activation meditation and was explaining the accelerated methods I had adopted to decalcify and detox fluoride from the pineal gland: (1) removing fluoride using turmeric and (2) meditating on the golden light as a tunnel around the third eye. (In addition, the current dense fields for our wireless devices also shut down the pineal. Yet another reason to use Quantum Sound to dispel damage from EMFs.)

It is a well-established fact that continual exposure to fluoride in our water and food creates a powerful block to third-eye activation, resulting in the inability to access higher consciousness. As my community craved this connection, my meditations were popular for their ability to bypass the lengthier fluoride detoxification process.

At times, I noticed a mismatch of energies. I would become impatient because I could see something in a client that was being deeply hidden and obscured from vision. For me it was like being sped up: my perception would occur more quickly. In some instances, I would feel out of sync with those around me. They weren't on the same wavelength, so to speak. They were seeing and feeling reality through a different lens. Maintaining the awakened state became a challenge for me when there was so little support from the outside.

During this phase and up to the present, I began to wake up very early, around 4:00 a.m., sometimes even earlier. It was how I would tune into my truth and maintain my sanity so that when the events of the day began, I would have established my center. I wasn't being swept around like a ship in a hurricane.

During these early mornings, which have continued until now, I would become aware of attending meetings with my guides and teachers and receiving specific instructions that I would write down or dowse.

For example, one of these instructions was writing this very book! It did not quite seem like the perfect time to do so, but I received the guidance anyway, and was told to do this as quickly as possible, as people need to read about this work in one place.

I have discovered since then that I can maintain the awakened state only by listening to and acting immediately upon the information of my guides and inner self. If I deviate from this information, I am exposed to events, people, and things that are not beneficial to maintaining the awakened state. That fact alone set me apart from the crowd, as my reality became quite nonlinear and I began to do things according to the whispers (however faint) of my inner self.

I can give you one very concrete example of this. I was invited to speak about our work in the fall of 2018 at a mansion in Malibu, California, in front of an audience of very special people. For some reason, my inner guidance said no. Although I attempted to get the organizer to arrange another date, they refused. So, I told them I could not do this. Everyone thought that perhaps I was engaged in self-sabotage or something like that. Even I checked this out, and the answer was no. On the very day that my presentation was scheduled to occur, Malibu was hit by wildfires and the entire town was evacuated.

Seeing into Another Dimension

My awakening has gradually allowed me to become a medium. During the night, when I am supposed to be sleeping, I am often woken up with visions of the spirits of the deceased. At times when the parent of a member of our tribe dies, I will be visited by that parent and given a message to convey to the tribe member. In one case, the mother of one of my clients came to me and told me that there was a box with some important information in the house. She told me exactly where in the living room the box was. When my client opened the box, she discovered some financial material related to a life insurance policy she was not aware of.

I was experiencing a quickening, a heightening of my vibration, and at times people in the third dimension seemed so confused, disoriented, and traumatized. I would wake up and just know stuff. But they were not always glorified visions of angels and beautiful celestial beings bearing gifts and uplifting messages like in the movies, or as represented by masters who have attained a platform on the world stage. It is downright disconcerting to know, feel, and experience this information at times. You see, the spirit world knows stuff we don't. Our ability to receive this information depends only on our openness at the time, and our willingness to serve the people who are in our lives. This is why true service is so important, but what is equally important is your self-care time, so that you can process this information without becoming too overwhelmed.

I can tell you, though, this information will assist you as a healer to perform your work outside the box and to serve your clients at a more profound and effective level of consciousness.

My pineal-gland activation didn't happen overnight. After shutting down at the age of three, it took years for me to regain full access to this sacred pathway. My access to higher consciousness developed in stages and in states. Even now, as I write this book, I am in a new stage of my awakening, channeling the relevant content to connect with you and to connect you to the significance of your journey. As the messenger, I am here to demonstrate how I have achieved this enlightenment for myself, and how you can too. It's important for your spiritual evolution, so you can expand consciousness for yourself and your community. It's like one of those old chain letters than used to be passed around in the 1980s, only a lot more relevant. I'm the messenger here to show you that ayahuasca journeys in Peru, ceremonies in India, and pilgrimages to the Egyptian pyramids are not necessary for you to awaken and be able to fully deliver your healing capabilities. In chapter 12, as a thank you, I include a link to a sound-frequency soundtrack that will activate your pineal gland.

It has been estimated that 99 percent of the population have a dormant third eye. Sounds a little scary, doesn't it? We are walking, unconscious zombies. Without our third eye being open, our heart will not be fully open either.

Awaken to Your Authentic Power

By opening the pineal gland fully, you access your full quantum potential. When the gland is detoxed and activated, you open the flow for the high-vibration frequencies that support your journey and your healing business.

By removing your emotional block and cleansing energetic interferences, a dormant third eye can be reactivated. Whether it's aroused by my pineal-activation soundtrack, through Voice Code Analysis, or by the Quantum Sound Miracle filling your home with an awakening vortex, those frequencies must be free-flowing for maximum energetic access. While there are quick-fix routes to get pineal activation, there needs to be action to support it.

Through intention-setting, free will, meditation, and time spent focusing on the space between the eyes, you assist focus in this re-stimulation.

It is important for you to realize that this is your choice, and that it takes energy and concentration to maintain this choice. It is partially a free-will choice and intention to awaken the dormant potential of the third eye. It takes concentration and commitment, and a willingness to listen to and follow the guidance of your higher self—your inner self—to keep you on track. I have found that maintaining the energy of the awakened state is more challenging than one would think. It is easy to lose this energy and be pulled back into the collective density. Being unwilling to listen and act from inner knowing seems to be a challenging obstacle for most.

You can also set commands before sleep, to see and remember what you need to know for the awakening of yourself and your clients. Third-eye activation is an often-overlooked key ingredient for gaining receptivity. There must be a focused intent to see without judgement and to remain open to all that flows your way.

When you learn to "tune in" in this way, you will open a gateway to quantum consciousness that will distinguish you as an intuitively gifted and sought-after healer-coach who is naturally of great service to your friends, family, clients, and community. This will expand your role and your innate capabilities. When your frequencies are flowing freely, you will be granted deep access to the recesses of your client's issues and problems, so you will know what you need to do to help them along the trail of their journey. It's like receiving an all-access pass to your favorite band—you can learn everything you need to know about your heroes (the good and the less good) when you can see and understand the dynamics and the motives behind their actions.

You have found this book because your heart yearns for this awakening. You have an innate sense that it will assist you in serving your community and hundreds, if not thousands, of people in their personal awakenings. My methods in this book are channeled to get you to fulfill that purpose without any further pain or blockages.

My third-eye awakening gave me insights into the true needs of my clients. Not the surface-level complaints they thought they had, but the deeper underlying issues that were holding them back. I gained clarity on how to deliver their truth, if it was in their best interests. Why not every time? You will have encountered this yourself: sometimes the person who needs healing isn't in a position of receptivity, no matter that they found and paid for your services. Healing must be in the realm of possibility in order for it to occur.

Reading the Akashic Records

Sometimes when I am watching the news and I see governments spending millions on investigations, I wonder why they don't simply read the Akashic records.

Your clients have given you the implicit and explicit permission to work with them. This means that, as necessary, you will be granted access to read their Akashic records in order to serve them better.

I recently fell asleep during a telephone reading, and the client told me I said, "You have stopped reading your Akashic records at night. It is disturbing your sleep and giving you nightmares."

Reading your clients' Akashic records allows you to understand the presenting issue in greater depth. While not quite cutting to the chase in the way Voice Analysis does, such a reading does help you decide on the most appropriate steps to take alongside their healing soundtrack. When you understand the true source of the problem, you can sidestep the trial and error.

When I am working with a client, I use the Akashic records to show me something that feels just outside my reach. They are a valuable tool that allows me to provide greater service to my clients. It's like being upgraded from a spade to a digger, to assist in getting them out of their trench of bad habits, old programming, and misguided beliefs. If your clients are open, you'll also be able to show them how to attain the awakened state themselves.

Though I don't walk around the streets randomly reading people's records, when I am working with them in any capacity, I will often take a glance or be shown something.

One little warning: some of the leading and most famous self-development gurus have not connected to their pineal glands and attained the awakened state. While they can be, and most often are, wonderful teachers who fill people with hope to fulfill their desires, they teach using logical principles that attract the masses. There is a place for them, in terms of the consciousness evolution, but it is worth considering whether the teachers you are connecting to and talking about are awakening or living in an awakened state.

The Power of Listening

Just like the tiny print on the side of a medication bottle, I must warn you that the awakened state has its side effects. As I mentioned earlier, your reality shifts when you're connected and conscious, and you might tend to behave a little differently at times. From my experience and that of my tribe, fame and money become less important, and your attention transfers to actions and experiences driven by integrity and clarity. Your desire to be of service and to make a difference only becomes more intense.

If you're nodding your head, ready for this consciousness shift, then I can share a tool to help you integrate it. What is important right now is to set the intention that you will always use your higher intuition to guide and assist those who are drawn to you. When you operate from this noble position, your intention will bear fruit. Take a moment to close your eyes, and for a few moments focus on sending golden light to the middle of your forehead, and state "I am open and awakened with love."

When you are writing, use the same statement: "Open and Awakened with Love."

Your divine intuition is your greatest gift as a human. It has been neglected for six thousand years, when the pineal was shut down due to over-intellectualization. Having the most brilliant minds on the planet running and creating things has not and will not evolve humanity. It is the subtle insight of consciousness and awakening that will guide humanity back to freedom.

In conclusion, in the words of my partner Robert Lloy, a man who has dedicated his life to bringing these technologies into form to awaken humanity,

> *The subtle body is the doorway to the physical body, the brain, and the emotions. The master control system of the body is the subtle body. Our mission here is to stimulate the subtle body. Stimulating the subtle body is like rebooting your hard drive. It is an evolutionary gift that focuses on a way to reboot the hard drive of your mental computer with no memory of your judgments of being beautiful, ugly, fat, smart, etc. This new technology is truly about self-empowerment and allowing everything to be rebooted and restored. It is that simple. I think it will help each person find their destiny.*

This is what activating your pineal gland is all about. You will have the ability to see, know, and fulfill your higher destiny effortlessly, flawlessly, and happily. The stories are in the very words of our clients, to help you feel what they felt, know what they now know, and experience this shift and transformation into a more awakened state of consciousness and being.

By doing this, you can attain much greater results in your own life and with your clients. More importantly, you will eventually return to a state of peace and happiness. After all, that is what being a great healer-coach is about, correct?

CHAPTER 8

Hack 5:
Repatterning through
Delta Deep Sleep

No one is playing with less than 5 hertz. It's not what you hear, it's what your soul feels.

Robert Lloy, inventor of Scalar Wave technology,
co-founder of Quantum Sound therapy

Restorative Delta Sleep

Unless you've inherited some magic gene that has afforded you a lifetime of deep sleep, chances are you've had nights, periods, or a history of sleep issues. You have felt the slog of your brain after a restless night, you've noticed the impact on your work and mood after a bout of insomnia, and you've witnessed the effects that sleeplessness has on those around you. The impact is not just physical, either. Did you know your empathy for your loved ones and your clients is diminished by poor-quality sleep?

As mentioned in chapter 4, delta is the brain state where restoration occurs. Nights without delta deprive your body of the opportunity to rest and heal, and the subconscious maintains its hold on those old blocks and patterns. Science is beginning to prove the impact of deep delta brain wave bursts during sleep. What Robert and I discovered, first intuitively, then clinically, with the help of Dr. Octavio Pino, was that the world of science was also busy validating the same theory. If you recall, Dr. Pino was the former University of Miami neurolinguist, brain researcher, and medical doctor who has dedicated his life to researching cutting-edge quantum brain research and the quantum dynamic field. He is both a scientist and a mystic who has meditated for over fifty years.

The scientific proof about attaining deep delta states during sleep is in—and it will take the researchers about four years to present the conclusive evidence. In addition, sleep research also indicates that we are spending less time in delta during sleep. Due to our addiction to technology devices, we are spending increasing time in the beta brain wave state and less time in the delta brain wave state. Yet delta is the "gold of sleep," whereby we truly rest, heal, rejuvenate, and repattern!

There is evidence and definitive proof of the impact of resting in a period of delta brain waves, which will be absolutely scientifically validated over the next five years. You already know how a night of unrest feels compared with the benefits of a deep, lucid sleep. You're also here with me, taking a quantum leap of faith in my intuition and experiments on delta brain wave entrainment. I've learned the importance of trusting my intuition and guidance, and I thank you for joining me with your faith in this, too.

Meeting Dr. Octavio Pino

It was with this guidance that Robert Lloy and I found ourselves driving Florida's Gold Coast to meet with Dr. Pino and two medical doctors who were flying in from a nearby island.

The discussion that ensued both enlightened us and paved a divergent path to our current work.

Dr. Pino has been involved in the evolution of our work since 2013. As I was driving to Nashville to attend my son Mike's graduation from his master's program in finance, Dr. Pino taught me about the significance of deep delta sleep, through which we learn, repattern, and in many ways heal from the challenges of our lives and body.

To this day, Dr. Pino lives with the Quantum Sound technology in his home in South Beach. In his enlightening words, "This is the only technology on the planet that teaches the quantum brain to function."

As a dedicated brain researcher, he has advised and taught us over the years. He experienced some of the earlier versions of our work and has been profoundly connected to and interested in its evolution. His profound love of science and spirituality has supported its evolution into this form. Dr. Pino's advice was to divide our soundtrack into two distinct soundtracks, one to support daytime activities, focus, and creativity, and one to support letting go into a deep, peaceful sleep. To simplify this, we call these soundtracks AM and PM. Dr. Pino elaborated that the brain and consciousness would be most receptive to the frequencies during sleep. Ironically, we are most productive when we sleep. A growing body of scientific evidence shows that our most regenerative and productive time is while we are sleeping in the deep delta brain wave state. This was the information I was intuiting also, so to receive confirmation, and also a shortcut to further our technology, was nothing short of inspirational.

Sleep research is consistently showing that the delta brain wave state is when we are most likely to regenerate, learn, and repattern ourselves. This includes healing from addictions, lifelong destructive patterns, and illnesses. So, although it may seem counterintuitive, if you are having problems in your life, science is showing that the answer is to sleep more. Teenagers the world over are breathing a sigh of relief! When the brain enters the deep delta brain wave states, cell regeneration occurs and our behaviors become repatterned.

Armed with Dr. Pino's inspired insight and his confidence in our technology, we raced home to begin working on the PM soundtrack. It was imperative that we create those perfect delta meditative waves, as exclusive to nighttime as the executive lounge is to first-class flyers.

In our line of work, it's getting more common to address sleep quality as a first port of call in resolving chronic issues, but consider this a reminder that you are examining the quality of your client's sleep cycle. Couple that exploration with the knowledge you're acquiring here about deep delta brain restoration, and you're gaining another weapon in your arsenal to address your clients' unresolved subconscious blocks and to help them gain entry to a different state of consciousness.

Specifically, when our brain goes into the deep delta brain wave states, we can regenerate cells and repattern our behavior and memories.

The Magic of Deep Delta Sleep

Consider this: when in deep delta, the entire body, mind, and subconscious are being regenerated, healed, and upwired. This also implies that delta recovery is the recipe for rejuvenation and repatterning.

This conversation with Dr. Pino and his colleagues provided one of those elusive *aha* moments. It was at this moment that I understood that the key that unlocks the door to all healing is in the deep delta states. This also means that the sleep deprivation humankind is currently experiencing due to our obsession with technology will in the long term have an adverse impact on health. Dr. Pino was also very clear that our clients would be most receptive to the restorative soundtrack of the Miracle during their deep delta sleep. This is why I usually recommend, during what I've begun to call the "entrainment phase," when someone is new to the technology, that they place the Miracle by their bed for the first three weeks so that they receive the impact fully. This will also retrain them to go into the deep delta brainwave state more frequently and remain there for longer periods. This is why some of our clients report that they actually need fewer hours of sleep to awaken feeling refreshed.

I might ask, if sleep is our most productive time of repatterning, then why are our cultural sleep habits moving toward less sleep?

The research is conclusive: the addiction to checking Facebook thirty times a day, or the obsession with sending cat pictures to cheer up friends, is increasing our time in beta—and our time out of restorative brain waves. Due to our obsession with technologies that keep us in perpetual beta brain wave states, we are spending more time in states of beta brain wave alertness and are vulnerable to the primitive brain response of fight, flight, or freeze. It is paradoxical that as we "progress," we are becoming more vulnerable to diseases related to inadequate delta sleep, which can automatically reboot our brain, cells, and emotional energy field.

Sleep research indicates that modern humans are sleeping less and, while sleeping, spending less time in delta and more time in beta brain wave states. Compared to sleep habits in the 1940s, our sleep time alone is one hour less per night. This is counterproductive, given the strain our ever-busy lifestyle imposes on us. We should all be demanding tools to help us reach delta during the night, yet this is barely raised as a helpful approach to increased well-being.

If you're a lifelong meditator like I am, you've experienced how alpha and theta brain states have impacted your body's chemistry—from the amygdala's fight-or-flight response to the parasympathetic nervous system. There are thousands of studies proving this effect. While meditating, you may also have noticed an increase in the chatter around you, especially as you strive to build your healer-coach business. The ability to quiet the monkey mind gets more challenging as life gets busier. It therefore makes sense that deep delta entrainment during sleep is another hack to resolve any issues. We all have those friends who say they are too busy to meditate, or that they cannot because of the chatter of their monkey mind. According to Dr. Pino, deep delta bypasses the day-to-day chatter and the "I can't meditate" mindset, providing the key to automatically open the door to repatterning and restoration.

When we add to the dense wireless fields that shut down the pineal, we are acting negligently toward a place not just of rest but also of future energy stores that we're going to need to succeed in reaching our goals. Although we believe that beta is where we are being most productive, it is actually in the deep delta states that we repattern, process, refuel, and integrate. According to Dr. Pino, delta is our most productive time on earth.

It is now five years since that life-changing meeting with Dr. Pino in Miami. Scientific research studies on sleep and delta brain waves continue to evolve at universities throughout the world. It is estimated that by 2022, the evidence will be conclusive on deep delta brain wave states being the key to healing and personal transformation.

In Dr. Pino's words,

How is the brain capable of downloading info that's around us, in the form of waves and frequencies? It's because we live in a world of information, light and energy.

The brain is not just the physical brain, the neurons, which you can dissect and observe. The brain goes beyond that, and interacts with the electromagnetic field around us.... And produces a field. The quantum brain exists as a hologram and has a vast field.

The area of the brain in the right hemisphere (which is capable of absorbing energy like an antenna) is more engaged when we're asleep and in meditation ... so it's more receptive to programming—because it works at the quantum level, with the subatomic particles which are also waves.

Your Brain Emanates a Field

So how does the quantum brain or consciousness resonate in the field of the iQube? Think quantum! As Dr. Pino states, the brain acts more like an antenna, picking up the signals from the "tuning fork" (the iQube), especially during the time of maximum receptivity (deep delta sleep). The iQube is acting like a lighthouse that is sending out signals to the brain (the boat). Once these signals are detected, there is a corresponding sympathetic attunement that allows a deeper level of sympathetic resonance. By emitting continual vibrations or frequencies that emanate into the environment, the iQube tunes the actual mind, spirit, and body to resonate and entrain with coherent frequencies; this results in greater clarity, harmony, and coherence.

There are two principles operating here: (1) the cleansing or vacuum effect of "sucking" out the negative or incoherent energies, and (2) the "feeding" effect of filling the cells of the body, the environment, with both coherent frequencies of sound and scalar energy that actually fill in the empty spaces of your cells, brain, and body with the highest "nutrition," in the form of frequencies, inert noble gases, and precious metals. These generate an alchemical field that you breathe in and absorb through your cells, in a sense feeding your body, soul, and brain.

I know this may sound a little out there and complex, but take a moment. Think quantum again! Visualize yourself standing in the rays of the sun as the sun rises. Visualize yourself absorbing the energy of the sun and neutralizing any of the negative effects you've gathered, such as radiation. This is the way Scalar Optimized Sound technology operates. It shines its "light" continuously and neutralizes and dissipates the lower frequencies of energy, like the stuck or frozen blocks that lie dormant in the subconscious, waiting to emerge. If these congestions of energy are dissolved, there is a loosening effect. I will call this loosening effect *transformation*. The discordant or incoherent vibrations are automatically released into the earth. This, of course, occurs primarily at the unconscious level. This is why we feel lighter, freer, as though the heaviness has just dissipated.

When the device emits the programmed frequencies, the person's brain waves entrain and enter into a state of wholeness known as *coherence*. Living within the coherent field created by the waves emitted by the iQube, one can create new neurological connections and learn new things. The enhanced neuroplasticity allows you to learn and absorb new information more efficiently.

Without making you switch off due to the trigger of quantum physics terminology, I will explain that the key to awakening your quantum brain lies in the quantum dynamic field. This is the multi-dimensional field that your brain field is constantly swimming in. Understanding this is alone sufficient to make a breakthrough in your awareness.

<<<|>>>

Pause for a moment. Take a few deep belly breaths and contemplate this: your brain is actually not a physical organ, it is a field. As a field, it is constantly interacting with the intangible field of your environment—most of which you cannot see, hear, taste, or smell. So you remain unconscious of the field you are swimming in.

<<<|>>>

Dr. Pino explains, "This iQube technology effectively trains the quantum brain by learning within resonance, at the frequency that is being input." The key according to Dr. Pino is that the technology is playing 24-7, which allows continual entrainment. The "field of the brain" remains in an entrainment phase throughout the day and night when in the presence of the iQube. This is indeed a difference, as most vibrationally based technologies allow only brief exposure that involve your voluntary engagement by lying on a mat or sitting on a specific lounge to receive stimulation.

He goes on to clarify that scalar energy resonates and trains your brain to be uplifted effortlessly into the field of pure consciousness while you work, play, rest, or meditate in your home or office environment.

Dr. Pino was impressed that the technology affords a lesson that so many do not know they need: how to sleep. Much as meditation was scoffed at in the early days, so too perhaps is the notion that you need to learn how to fulfill such a basic human need as sleep. This is as significant a concept to awaken in people as a belly breath was a few years ago.

When you learn how to sleep entrenched in the quantum field, you are bathed in a sea of pure energy. It's a cellular overhaul that is far more influential when you're asleep than awake. The technology provides the reboot that you probably didn't know you needed, but once you experience it, you are quickly introduced to its power.

Delta sleep is important. It moves you to the next level, not only to sleep better but also to release, reboot, and repattern the subconscious—the memories of the past as well as the present.

As Dr. Pino continued to explain, "Therefore, delta sleep is so important. You must teach them this." So this is exactly what I am doing here!

The irony is that, in his words, "You will not remember what goes on in deep delta." So how can this be so healing? What goes on in deep delta is a bit of a mystery, but in this state you are most likely to repattern persistent beliefs and to heal.

Go Deeper for a Moment

Let's breathe into the belly and observe what brain wave state you are in at this time.

One of the things you could do is measure how long you sleep in the delta brain wave state. A search for *sleep* in Apple's App Store reveals over five thousand apps.

One of the great benefits of delta deep is that when you wake, while you will not remember what has occurred, you will feel more deeply rested and refreshed. You will sleep without waking for longer periods and you will wake more rested. You will experience the benefits of the delta brain wave state in every area of your waking life—health, mood, patience, recall, ideation.

While you are in deep delta, you are more receptive and susceptible to *subtle energy*. What do I mean by subtle energy? This is composed of the nuanced frequencies we cannot measure with our contemporary forms of measurement. Even in the physical realm, you will experience the effects following the delta sleep session. After waking from a delta sleep session, you may witness an uplifting of your mood, and over time you will notice changes in lifelong behavior and personality patterns, or shifts in your vision of reality. I have had clients experience paradigm shifts in medical diagnoses that doctors have considered unfathomable. It is not within the scope of this book to discuss these paradigm shifts; suffice it to say that when harmony is restored at the physical, mental, emotional, and spiritual vibratory levels, there is a quantum potential for miracles to unfold effortlessly. These can be in the form of paradigm shifts and changes in diagnoses.

Cats Hang Out by the Miracle

Being more attuned to frequency and vibrations than us mere humans, cats are naturally drawn to the Quantum Sound Miracle. There is evidence that they know how to align with the magnetic fields of the earth to heal themselves.

There are many stories of pet healings with our technology. For instance, I know of cats scheduled for expensive surgery for cancer who cured themselves of their condition, making the surgery unnecessary.

Cats in particular like to hang out around the Miracle iQube and seem quite capable of healing themselves! They are expert sound energy healers. It seems they are often ahead of us in trusting that healing is a vibrational activity. The significant difference here is that pets seem to be able to just relax and enjoy what "feels" good to them. They simply don't "overthink" it or feel too busy to just stretch out and enjoy the feelings of well-being when they bathe in this pool of delicious, coherent energy.

Our Secret Formula for Enhancing Your Neuroplasticity

Neuroplasticity is as on-trend now as celery, ketogenic diets, and ice baths. Author, lecturer, researcher, and educator

Joe Dispenza is a longtime advocate of rewiring the brain to alter and optimize your quantum potential. Back in the day, however, using brain wave entrainment for that process was considered untenable.

As I have mentioned, I have paranormal gifts, including clairaudience. Perhaps this is why, as I drifted off to sleep one night, I heard the delta frequency. This was before the enlightenment of the Miracle as a 24-7 tool and before we had developed the six waveforms that allow us to hear this inaudible sound. Delta frequency played out like an auditory hallucination, as strange as smelling a color.

When I went to sleep, I heard the frequencies (there was no technology on anywhere in the townhouse) in my own brain—like an auditory hallucination—a gift of my clairaudience. I called Les Marshall, our brainiac software designer, the next day to tell him of my experience. This is when Robert and I had the *aha* moment and realized what Les had accomplished.

Les explained that he had created a new waveform frequency that was essentially binaural beats tripled. We now affectionately call this hybrid waveform the Golden Six. The extensive research that Les explored in the Stanford University neuroscience journals and the Monroe Institute pointed to the brain's love for complex waveforms and diversity. Whereas most humans believe they feel most comfortable with the status quo, the brain is seeking an entirely different experience. Like a truck driver scanning the radio for an interesting talk show, the brain is constantly seeking novel information to excite and stimulate neuronal development. New frequencies can act almost as adrenaline, stimulating the formation of new synapses and greater neuroplasticity. When you have enhanced neuroplasticity, you are smarter, more intuitive, and have a greater ability to draw from the resources of the environment.

Normally, you do not hear delta frequencies, as they are below the average range of human hearing. However, with Les's waveform breakthrough, the combination of the six waveforms, the harmonics, and the overtones allowed the delta frequencies to be picked up and heard. I admit that at times this waveform, which beats six frequencies together simultaneously, sounds a bit unusual. At times it even sounds like static, and to the untrained ear not used to these odd sounds, it may seem as if something is wrong. This is because our work is frequency-based, and as such it is not designed to sound like harmonious music. Over a period of time, which I like to call the entrainment phase, people adjust to these odd sound formulas. Later, a German audio inventor created a dedicated amplifier that allowed delta to be felt and experienced. This has greatly enhanced our technology, as people resonate greatly when they can feel and experience delta brain waves throughout the body. It impacts the sensation of truly restful sleep when using the Miracle.

While you are sleeping in deep delta, you may be cruising the universe in search of your next brilliant insight, something to support and help your clients grow and heal, or in search of ways to help your child do better in school. This is what the Golden Six Waveform Soundtracks accomplish, by teaching the brain to optimize its native neuroplastic abilities.

The result of this is that one of the first things I hear from people who receive their Quantum Sound Miracles is that they are sleeping more deeply and feel more refreshed than ever before.

Harvard's Deep Delta Sleep Research

Deep delta sleep is a marker for biological youth, thanks to its regenerative qualities. Delta has a regenerative quality that can even improve your memory. Sleep researcher Dan Gartenberg, PhD, teamed up with Dmitry Gerashchenko, MD, PhD, from Harvard Medical School to research the impact on health and well-being of deep delta brain wave states during sleep.

Is it possible that your sleep is not as regenerative as it could be? What if you could make your sleep more regenerative? Have you noticed that nowadays it's almost like a badge of honor to not get enough sleep? Our culture is so intent on proving our busyness and how few hours we spend in bed that we wear this burden with pride.

Thankfully, sleep researchers and advocates for sleep health are changing this with awareness of the health hazards of sleep deprivation. For example, if you do not treat a diagnosis like sleep apnea, you are more likely to suffer a stroke or get Alzheimer's disease, heart disease, or cancer (to mention just a few health challenges).

Dr. Dmitry Gerashchenko shared a fascinating piece of research in which a lab in Germany demonstrated that if they played certain sounds at the right time during sleep, they could actually increase the depth of a person's sleep and improve the sleep's restoration results. Added to this, the lab showed that they could improve next-day memory performance with the same sound.

Dr. Octavio Pino's Insights

Dr. Pino had just returned from Ganeshpuri, India. I called him while he was standing outside the meditation temple he goes to regularly in Miami. His message to me was "Helena, you need to teach modern people how to sleep, breathe, and love."

He then went on to clarify that it was difficult to measure the full impact of the Miracle technology, as it affects intangible subtle energy. Science in the West does not have an effective way of measuring subtle energy. This is an odd paradox, as Dr. Pino is very good friends with the Russian scientist and inventor Konstantin Korotkov, PhD, who has developed tools and technology to measure subtle energy. You can review a sample of the before-and-after chakra photos taken with Dr. Korotkov's machine (two photos are included in chapter 5) when you visit the Quantum Sound Therapy website at quantumsoundtherapy.com.

Dr. Pino also stated that our technology creates the quantum dynamic field that the leading philosophers, sages, and gurus of our time create at their events. There would be less need to attend these events if attendees slept, lived, and breathed in the field of our Quantum Sound technology.

We have learned from hundreds of clients' reports that we could support the production of deep, regenerative delta brain waves by playing the sounds—even inaudibly—through the Quantum Sound technology.

Playing the right sounds (deep delta brain waves) during sleep facilitates the optimal sound environment and sleep habitat. The brain is most receptive during sleep. It is the subtle energy field of the brain that entrains with the frequencies and the waves generated. This will automatically improve people's sleep health and their overall health, well-being, and adaptation to stress.

Arianna Huffington, inspirational leader and founder of the *Huffington Post*, is no stranger to sleep issues. After burning the candle at both ends, she collapsed in her office from sleep deprivation. She went on to write the insightful and brilliant book *The Sleep Revolution: Transforming Your Life, One Night at a Time*. In essence, she writes that even though we know more about sleep now than at any other time in history, and even though we know how important deep sleep is to our well-being, getting enough sleep is harder to do than ever. As I say earlier in this chapter, when you search *sleep* in the Apple Store, you find five thousand apps. Fifteen million photos pop up when you search *#sleep* on Instagram. Twenty-four million images appear when you search *#tired* on Instagram. A Google search on the word *sleep* will bring up over 800 million results! So we are sleep-obsessed and sleep-deprived at the same time!

> *Sleep is a time of intense neurological activity—a rich time of renewal, memory consolidation, brain and neurochemical cleansing, and cognitive maintenance. Properly appraised, our sleeping time is as valuable a commodity as the time we are awake. In fact, getting the right amount of sleep enhances the quality of every minute we spend with our eyes open.*
>
> Arianna Huffington,
> *The Sleep Revolution: Transforming Your Life,*
> *One Night at a Time*

Over time, the effects of sleep deprivation can have a significant impact on our ability to function in our jobs, to maintain and enrich our relationships, and to favorably affect our overall state of well-being.

Delta Brainwave Benefits

How have your sleep patterns impacted your output, both personally and professionally? Here is a list of reasons to entrain with our delta waves 0–4 Hz soundtrack:

- ✓ Delta waves are the deepest level of meditation.
- ✓ The delta state is associated with no thinking during deep, dreamless sleep.
- ✓ Delta brain waves are very rewarding.
- ✓ Delta waves are said to be the entrance to non-physical states of reality.
- ✓ The delta state is crucial for renewal, healing, and rejuvenation.
- ✓ The immune system strengthens in the delta state.
- ✓ Delta waves are linked to the unconscious part of our mind.
- ✓ Many scientists believe delta waves to be the most beneficial brain waves.

CHAPTER 9

Hack 6:
High-Vibe Structured Water

Since the molecular structure of water is the essence of all life, the man who can control that structure in cellular systems will change the world.

Albert Szent-Gyorgi,
author of *Bioelectronics: A Study in Cellular Regulations, Defense, and Cancer.*
Nobel Prize Winner

Water is indeed the basis of a new quantum science. Basic biology and health are poised for a revolution. Liquid crystalline water is the key. Water has always been thought of as boring stuff. But water is (now) at the center stage of cell biology and medicine, consciousness. It's all down to water.

Mae-Wan Ho, PhD,
author of *Living Rainbow H2O*

Masaru Emoto Is on a Mission

Why did Masaru Emoto, author of the *New York Times* bestseller *The Hidden Messages in Water*, travel half-way around the world to track us down in Oxnard, California?

How did this pivotal historic moment happen, when two of the grandfathers in the structured-water movement came together?

It was February 12, 2003, and Masaru Emoto was on a mission to find Robert Lloy and explore how he could apply Robert's Scalar Wave technology to create a stable structured-water formula as a flagship for his own work. Emoto had heard about Robert and his research and work through a renowned Japanese neurosurgeon, Naoki Shibuya.

We were sitting in our home in Oxnard, California, when we received Dr. Emoto's call. He'd come to ask us for help with his mission.

Dr. Emoto kept saying, "This is an historic day."

Together, we were about to discover the visual impact that imprinting within the zero-point energy field has on the hexagonal geometry of living water. We were going to figure out how to make healing water that makes people happier and more whole.

Dr. Emoto's global quest to track us down marked the beginning of our long and fruitful journey together. As Dr. Emoto later wrote in his newsletter:

> *It was an historical event. On February 12, 2003, I traveled to Oxnard, California, to attend a meeting with Robert Lloy to discuss his Scalar Wave Technology and how he could apply it to create an excellent Structured Water*

for me in my global work. At this historical meeting, I presented Mr. Lloy with the crystalline photography of his structured water formulas. Later that year, I invited Robert Lloy to form a partnership which I named EmLloy in honor of our surnames, Emoto and Lloy. Mr. Lloy has invented a complex technology and corresponding manufacturing facility which is capable of imprinting coherent frequency information into water, using his zero-point energy field technology.

The mission and intent of the partnership was and continues to be to provide humanity with high-frequency structured water to raise a person's vibration, one cell at a time, while uplifting their consciousness to the frequency of love.

Dr. Shibuya had been applying our Scalar Wave technology at his neurosurgery clinic, with excellent results. Dr. Shibuya had read, seen, and understood the potential implications for his research. So much so, he wrote *The Gift*. This nine-hundred-page title was only available in Japanese. I believe it is out of print now and has not yet been translated into any other languages.

Emoto's Dilemma ... and Our Unique Solution

Even in those early days, around the turn of the twenty-first century, Masaru Emoto had made the quantum leap in his understanding that structured water is most easily absorbed by the cells because it provides true hydration. The reduced size of a water molecule that is structured to be hexagonal in shape allows it to penetrate the cells and hydrate more efficiently. Emoto also understood that the secret key to creating perfectly hexagonal water concentrates lies in first creating a stable structured water molecule.

What he hadn't found yet in his search was a source of stable structured water. In his extensive research, Dr. Emoto had been experimenting with photographing many possible sources of hexagonal water—including our technology, which created beautiful hexagonal water molecules.

Here for your contemplation are pictures of our water, delivered on the historic day of the EmLloy partnership. You can visit our website at quantumsoundtherapy.com/structured-water to view some of the images that Dr. Emoto took of our structured water formulas and to read more about our journey with him. I'd like to take a moment to thank the late Masaru Emoto for the invaluable contribution he made to our work. All of the images on our structured-water bottles are images supplied by Dr. Emoto.

Dr. Emoto realized that our hexagonal water is similar in structure to the healing water of Lourdes, which he had studied extensively. It's been well established in the scientific community studying water that the structure of Lourdes's healing water only holds its hexagonal shape for about twenty minutes. Once removed from its source, it quickly loses its unique geometry and healing power. The crux of our relationship and success with Dr. Emoto lies here: our structured water can travel thousands of miles and remain perfectly imprinted.

Through our work with noted water scientist Dr. Lee Lorenzen, the Harmony Water that we created for Dr. Lorenzen's company was perfectly hexagonal, stable, and crystalline. At no point does our water lose its potency, unlike the water at Lourdes. It was a significant breakthrough, and our structured water was deemed by Dr. Emoto to be the highest-quality stable structured water available on the planet.

The Key Is in the Geometry

The purpose of imprinting water is, in short, to change the geometry of water from *incoherent* (unstable and unstructured) to *coherent* (stable, structured, organized, and six-sided, like the water channels of your cells). This way your cells can absorb the water more quickly and easily.

Using our Scalar Wave imprinting process, every water molecule is packed tight with information to deliver coherent frequency information that uplifts and supports your vibration and desired transformation. If humans are between 60 and 70 percent water, then absorbing harmonious water is surely one of the most impactful ways to raise your frequency, all while drinking water! No longer can people deem water a boring drink, when you can get high vibes with every sip.

Drinking Crystalline-Frequency Water Is a Hack

Drinking crystalline-frequency water is a hack to greater coherence and healing. It is absorbed directly into the cellular bio-matrix. Could it be better than drinking fresh celery juice? Structured water is different from ordinary water, as the imposed structure forms hexagonal water molecules that resemble a honeycomb. This actually balances the pH. The best way to measure the balancing of pH is to measure the urine before and after drinking structured water; pH paper strips are readily available.

Hexagonally structured water appears to play an important role in biological functions. One of the greatest pioneers in structured water, Dr. Mu Shik Jhon, has this to say:

> *In the human body, structured and disordered water exist at the same time, and we have shown that the body's survival rate decreases as the amount of disordered water accumulates. The greater the amount of structured water in the body, the healthier an individual is, and it is not likely that disease will invade the healthy body. Once again, an important key to health is the amount of hexagonally structured water we have in our bodies. In the end the one with the most Hexagonal Water wins!*

Water Has Memory

The scientific work of the late French immunologist Jacques Benveniste also holds a clue to the mystery of water. After many years of research, Benveniste concluded that water does indeed hold memory. This means that whatever frequency you place in water is remembered. This is great news for those of us who take the time to "structure" water, as it implies that even if the water "forgets," it can be reminded simply by lowering the temperature or freezing the water.

Dr. Benveniste's work was highly controversial during his lifetime. Although he could have received a Nobel Peace Prize, he was criticized and condemned by his colleagues. Now his work is recognized by the scientific community as having some substance. There are several short films on YouTube about his research laboratory. The key to understanding this, though, is that water remembers everything, so if it has been through the toilet pipes a thousand times during its lifetime, it remembers the signature of this as well!

This does make the process of finding and creating stabilized structured water more challenging, because water generally reverts to holding earlier memories from before the structuring process.

It was this challenge that eventually led Dr. Emoto to travel halfway around the world to meet with us. Due to the seventeen-stage process we use, our structured water was the only kind Emoto could find that holds the memory of coherent geometry. This, of course, is due to the properties inherent in our Scalar Wave imprinting technology.

Dr. Emoto wanted to know whether water could be imprinted with specific frequency information that would raise a person's resonance and facilitate a positive state of health. Could it work as an energy hack for harmony, balance, and relaxation?

Coherent Flow at Group Events

For the past few years, I have been traveling and assisting some consciousness leaders, coaches, and healers during their events, where we share our structured-water formulas and Quantum Sound technology with the participants. Depending on the events and the intended outcome, our structured water is provided to increase the focus of the group (Miracle Water), to help balance the left with the right brain (Indigo Water), or to increase consciousness (Spirit Molecule).

I've witnessed firsthand the increased frequency of the group drinking our water, and I am always invited back by the event leaders, as they have been able to effectively share their message with more receptivity and clarity. The water makes the event more fluid (pun intended) and enhances happiness, group coherence, and communication.

After one event, I overheard the audience demanding the water, sounding like chocoholics locked outside a candy store. They had felt so good during that day's event that they wanted that buzz to continue.

Thankfully, our structured water is a "message in a bottle," which they can, and do, take home with them (or to the party). Though I don't have the space in this chapter to go over our observations in detail, I will summarize what we have collectively observed:

- ✓ There is a lightness and receptivity that automatically unfolds in the group.
- ✓ People seem more capable of receiving the information being shared.
- ✓ Groups have longer attention spans.
- ✓ There is more happiness and satisfaction with the results from the event.
- ✓ There is greater communication and sharing among participants.

This has shown me that the coherent waves imprint people's cells with frequency information in a way that can be more impactful than words. In a sense, the frequency of the water being imbibed supports and amplifies the high-vibration shift that the leader is modeling.

These frequencies are saturating the cells with coherence in such a way that it supports the desired outcome of the group, event, or individual. What I've felt and experienced personally is a lightening of the emotions and a dampening of the left-brain critic.

When people approach me with serious left-brain questions such as "Why this?" or "How that?," I often pull out a bottle of our structured water concentrate—like Spirit Molecule formula, based on dimethyltryptamine (DMT), a naturally occurring hallucinogen—and propose we do micro-dosing shots together. Unlike a shot of tequila or Jägermeister, these are quality shots of high-frequency information. Does it get any better than that? I pour out these one-ounce shots and we drink them together, like a bar ritual. Like in a bar, we end up laughing, but we also join our energies and see the light and love in it all. This conscious high-energy drinking bonds us. I can see some of the people's doubts vanish as their hearts open. The hangover is way better, too.

What people really want, and what you are really asking me to deliver, is this: an expanded sense of freedom, lightness, and heart-opening joy. Can this be transmitted through a coherent water molecule that has been imprinted for seventy-two hours? Hell, yeah!

I've seen thousands of people relax and become happier as they imbibe our structured water. The human body is 70 percent water, 60 percent of which is found inside the cells and 40 percent outside the cells. It is estimated that our blood is approximately 83 to 90 percent water. Water is essential to our physical and emotional well-being, and we've found one quantum way to amplify and upgrade how we use it.

Rejuvenation through a Return to Bio-Water?

According to the late, renowned water expert Dr. Mu Shik Jhon, the water in the body of a newborn is 100 percent bio-water—naturally structured, hexagonal water. The natural hexagonal structure of the water decreases as we age and is replaced with disorganized (unstructured) water. As we age, our bodies do not produce any additional bio-water. By age fifty, less than 50 percent of our water is bio-water.

Aging also brings with it the challenge for water to cross the cell membrane walls to rehydrate us. From this perspective, cell water turnover and the presence or lack of hexagonal water in the body become critical markers for wellness, health, and longevity. Structured hexagonal water is the scientifically created form of bio-water. As the human body cannot produce bio-water on its own after birth, we must consume hexagonally structured water for it to reach our cells. This knowledge—that imbibing structured water improves aging and health—is yet another key to unlocking the ideal bio-terrain for improved health. It is our sixth Quantum Hack.

More importantly, coherent water molecules have the ability to carry high-frequency information that supports your body's quantum transformation. They can deliver directly to the cells the vibrations that can open your heart and activate your mind, as well as give you a natural experience of the DMT molecule. The body creates its own DMT to alter and raise your perception.

Our structured water creates a doorway to the microcosmic quantum terrain, delivering packets of high-frequency information to penetrate your cells and raise their frequency, and that of your energy field. It can also increase your body's capacity to absorb nutrition.

When we imprint our structured water, we always imprint the water molecule—even the water molecules in the air. Of course, you cannot see these; neither can you see into the bioterrain of your cells.

Our Unique Imprinting Process

In 2007, we moved our water plant from Ventura, California, to Hot Springs, Arkansas. Of course, everyone thought we were a little crazy, but it was all quite intentional. We had visited every water plant in Southern California, and Robert and I had co-created a beautiful energy plant in one of Ventura's office parks. We had learned, however, that since water has an amazing memory and picks up and retains the frequencies and vibrations of everything it comes into contact with, even though we were using a distilled water base our water was still carrying many previous memory frequencies.

Let us go deeper, to the source. Think about it with me for a moment. Water travels through pipes in walls and remembers what it is exposed to. It has an infinite capacity to remember. This means that exposure to excreted pharmaceuticals is recycled into water tanks—regular testing shows that 1 out of every 8 cups of tap water is a cocktail of designer pharmaceuticals. If we drink, or even cook with, tap water, this "signature," or vibratory frequency, is carried into our cells.

We chose a location nine miles away from the legendary Mountain Valley Spring Water manufacturing facility, where the water is pumped out in abundance daily from a spring deep within the recesses of the earth. As it turns out, these springs are considered to be in the top three in the US. Many naturopaths recommend that their clients have this spring water shipped to them at their homes. This water has never traveled the terrain of Los Angeles or Ventura County water. Our water is as clean and pure as any source of water on earth today, so it provides us with a clean base. We purchase the base distilled and then proceed to do a seventy-two-hour scalar-frequency imprinting process. The frequencies are subtle, of course, so it is necessary to use a distilled base, so that the hard particles do not interfere with the frequency information.

Let me share how powerful this water can be. In 2011, we were approached by a detective, Terry, who owned a golf-clothing company. He asked if we could imprint his clients' clothing to see whether it could affect their performances in their golf games. It was an interesting concept, but not aligned with our purpose or mission, and I told Terry this. Even so, I said I would investigate it. We had been meticulously developing our water-imprinting process for twenty years, so it took a great deal of prompting and persuasion before we agreed to develop a protocol for Terry. He knew what he wanted and he kept calling me, eventually deciding to visit.

We agreed to place Terry's 100-percent cotton or hemp t-shirts on our quantum technology and spray them with our structured water. We shipped them back to Terry's office. Terry discovered a point-of-sale machine that measured balance and acuity and tested the t-shirts. Quite to our surprise, our quantum imprinting process very effectively increased the balance and golf swing of whoever wore the imprinted t-shirts.

When Terry visited us, he brought a friend who was on the board of the Bill and Melinda Gates Foundation. At that time, the Gates Foundation was sending frozen vaccines overnight to third-world countries. They were losing millions of dollars because the ice was not keeping the vaccines cold enough to remain viable. Losing vaccines in this way was impacting many lives. Thanks to the visit by this Gates Foundation representative, we worked with the Foundation, using our structured water for the ice. They found that it froze faster and stayed frozen longer, ensuring safe delivery of the life-altering vaccines. These vaccines remained viable and delivered amazing results.

Our structured water was also tested for moist-curing concrete in the city of Detroit. The engineers found that they needed 20 percent less water than usual, and that the concrete was harder, with our structured water.

These stories highlight the impact of coherent water molecules and their power to alter every biological process in your body and your mind.

If you would like to delve more deeply into the subject of structured water formulas, visit our product page for Quantum Structured Water at quantumsoundtherapy.com/structured-water.

CHAPTER 10

Hack 7:
Take Back Your Power

The idea of vibrating each cell of the mind-spirit-body complex into a higher form of expression is not new and transcends the ideas of religion.

Gregg Braden,
The Divine Matrix

Healing the Healer

*M*any seekers, healers, and coaches blame themselves for their failure to fully actualize the teachings from self-development events. They actually feel a profound sense of shame and loss, as though it is their fault they haven't automatically imbibed and acted upon what they were learning. Yet there are some very specific reasons for this, and when understood, they are so simple.

It is truly a roller-coaster ride for so many people. The spouse may sit at home and observe the roller coaster and wonder, "Why you are seeking externally?" It may even make them feel like a failure.

Have you ever helped take down the set after the self-development event is over? It is like the entire energy vanishes, and the space returns to the vacuous energy of the hotel; the chairs are removed or go back into place, and the monotonous color and design of the hotel returns. Where did that exuberant, vibrant, full-of-life-and-vitality energy go? It went out the door with the leader and the group.

The energy of the leader and the group acts like hypnosis, inducing a trance state. At a snap of the fingers, voila! You are back in that state. Most highly successful self-development leaders are studying the impact of certain structures on your behavior, by the way. Both act as a form of hypnosis, and you enter the trance state when you enter stage left.

Let's look at it in terms of a stage, props, and a movie. The environment the leader created—the people, the structure, the audible teachings, the practices—is no longer present at your home. The props only reinforced new behavior while you were there. They were part of the field that was entraining you.

These events promise the world, but in the end, when you return home, it is you who returns home.

When you return home, there is another stage: your environment—what you have previously created. This environment that you live in automatically retrains you back to who you were before the event. Your children, your partner, your kitchen, your pets are excellent entrainment reminders that bring you back to the memory of who you were before the event. Both locations are carefully constructed (or perhaps not-so-consciously constructed, in the case of your home) quantum dynamic fields that entrain you to be a certain way. What would happen if we altered your home environment so that it was a conscious quantum dynamic field that automatically upwired your behavior and the behavior of those you love—of your food, pets, clothing, plants? The very subtle energy field that you and your conscious brain live in?

This is what we have mastered with our work: it influences the quantum field to consciously create an environment in your home and office that automatically and consistently envelops you in coherent sound waves, raising your resonance even while you are sleeping.

I can assure you there is no reason for guilt, being hard on yourself, or beating yourself up. The secret lies in understanding your brain. Your brain is always seeking to keep you alive. It will always return to what it finds safe, until you provide it with new coherent or intelligent information to entrain with and learn from. That is the simple secret that is the pillar of our approach.

The change you are seeking has to occur and be supported 24-7 within your own brain, consciousness, and environment rather than in some hotel room three thousand miles away from where you live. Otherwise, you live on this constant roller coaster of high emotions followed by crashes.

Are you grasping the paradoxical nature of this behavior? You need to feed the brain, body, and soul new coherent information in the everyday context that you live, work, and breathe within—you need to rewire and upwire. This can be done in the context of your primary healing modality.

We are giving the brain and the consciousness new information to learn from, by generating a subtle energy field composed of coherent sound waves that will instruct, inform, and fill the space. Your brain will automatically entrain with the coherent sound waves—just as you do when you are at an event.

The Quantum Miracle iQube is like your portable uplifting self-development in a box. It emanates waves of high-frequency, coherent information and love, opening you gently to the waves of love and light that are within you and your office or environment, instead of in some hotel space that you will leave

Let the music begin again. The dance and the rhythm of the dance continue as the ineffable reminders that you can only really push the edge of the envelope back at home with Miracle support. Your partner (husband, wife, child, mother, or client) didn't attend with you. Those beautiful sound bites of knowledge and energy that you received seem to vanish into thin air until the next shiny object appears, promising you endless happiness and transformation ... if you will only attend the next event.

<<<|>>>

Take a moment to breathe deeply into your belly at least three times. This will automatically take you out of the amygdala brain and relax you into the parasympathetic nervous system.

So Many Modalities in the Newtonian Worldview

The "healing trap" is the belief that somewhere outside yourself there lies a solution to the feeling that you are not whole. It says that, ultimately, if you study your primary modality more deeply, take enough personal-development courses, meditate, do yoga, go to the gym, and eat a raw vegan diet, you will find the solution that makes you whole.

Many have bankrupted themselves in this quest and remain painfully incomplete in their quest for wholeness and perfection.

The gift of quantum physics, and the philosophy of *The Quantum Doctor*, is that all modes of healing are complementary and included. In the words of the book's author, Amit Goswami, PhD, "In quantum physics, what we normally perceive as 'things' are seen to be not things; instead they are seen to be possibilities for consciousness to choose from."

This idea has the power to integrate all the diverse philosophies underlying the mechanics of the many branches of alternative medicine and healing. This inclusive philosophy is uniquely grounded in the age of enlightenment that we are entering into.

I have met so many alternative healer-coaches who have obtained endless certifications for this modality and that modality. And though each is a piece of the puzzle, and they all enhance each other, each must be remembered and applied. Subconsciously, we seem to feel incomplete and seek out solutions in the forms that are presented to us. Each represents an energetic waveform, a school of thought and a belief system. They are just different pathways to the same inevitable destination—ultimately, the global healing of humanity and of each individual currently resonating on planet earth! That is our true destination.

This is the supreme paradox. Each so-called modality is its own world. Despite the number of certifications you have, you may feel incomplete. You may continue to branch out, getting more qualifications in this or that esoteric form of energy healing or assessment, but as these certificates pile up on your wall, you still do not feel complete.

I have realized the reason for this feeling of incompleteness is that each healing branch or modality still conforms in some way to the Newtonian allopathic model, no matter how paradoxical that seems. The allopathic model seeps in and takes over the modality. We know why. This Newtonian model is deeply rooted in our conscious and subconscious minds, and in the collective consciousness. The "healer" is doing the "healing." The "client" goes to see the "healer" to obtain a new frame of reference, and hopefully something within or without is altered, transformed, or as we like to call it in the old paradigm, healed. *In the new paradigm that is upon us, I like to say, "The client has resonated to a new frequency," or "harmonized."*

Most healing modalities deal with the physical body as an object to be manipulated, treated, and healed. But they are painfully incomplete. Why? Because they do not consider the quantum dynamic field—the actual energy field that we are living in, breathing from, and swimming in. They do not consider the waveforms that surround us and envelop us. Even if they do consider the energy field of the body, they don't consider the sound waves that create the fields of our homes, bedrooms, living rooms, sanctuaries, offices, and highways.

Why is this? Because most of the founders, creators, and inventors of these modalities working in the alternative healing industry today have not attained awakening themselves. On some level, they are not awakened. Many of these modalities come from a certain body of experience, and from the mind. These are mental constructs.

What I would like to make you aware of, because I do love you and care about you (you are part of the whole), is that this feeling of incompleteness is coming from the old paradigm.

We live in a world of vibration and sound waves. Once this is fully realized, truly fully realized, we will have collectively shifted into a new paradigm of transformative healing, coaching, and living.

We are still in the transition from the old materialistic, Newtonian paradigm that created the allopathic model of medicine. This has infiltrated most people's way of thinking, feeling, and being in this world. I know that you know this.

To summarize briefly, in the Newtonian paradigm, the world is composed of physical, solid objects that are measurable.

The Quantum Paradigm

The new paradigm is one based on the quantum vision of reality. Everything is in vibration and is instantly changeable. The world of subatomic particles (the quantum world) is always in flux. The laws governing subatomic particles are multi-dimensional, meaning that, for example, a subatomic particle can appear in three thousand places at once, as I mention in chapter 3. The perceiver of the subatomic, or quantum, particle can affect and impact the particle. So, the laws governing the new vibrational paradigm are totally different from Newtonian laws.

Also, everything you are looking at is actually nothing—empty space on the time-space continuum. You are no-thing, sitting on empty space in a continuum of time. That is the quantum or multidimensional reality.

We are all vibrations in resonance with one another. The living world is empty space we fill with our vibrations, thoughts, and subconscious beliefs. What manifests in your reality is your subconscious. Your subconscious beliefs hold a frequency, a resonance. As we are frequency beings who are manifest for a limited time as human beings, your subconscious can be altered during your brief sojourn on earth so that you can manifest more of what you desire.

Until you accept that you are frequency, and everything around you is frequency, and frequency is measurable and convertible, you are stuck in the belief or mindset that you are matter, which is not as adaptable.

Know this: your frequency can be upwired. And so can your resonance. And so can your brain.

There is significant evidence that we match frequencies, like veritable tuning forks, aligning with what surrounds us. In the case of the healer-coach, the optimal scenario is that your clients match your frequency and resonate with your frequency or higher.

Your brain and the field that you dwell in can be upwired and rewired

The frequency space that we share can be designed and altered. It is not difficult. Why? Because we have created a hack for it.

Thirty-Day Test

If you are serious about shifting your frequency so you can manifest a thriving life and healer-coach business, filled with joy and positive energy, I propose a thirty-day experiment with my 7 Quantum Hacks. I'm sure you can admit that parts of this book have highlighted areas of your life where your subconscious has been driving the bus, like Sandra Bullock in *Speed*. It's out of control, but it can be managed. It's time to step up and take the wheel back.

Maintaining a high frequency is crucial to being able to deliver great results as you move along your life-purpose path. When you practice any of my hacks, you'll notice greater resonance with your clients and improved results. Stay alert, wait, then watch!

You Are the Frequency Leader

You are the frequency leader for yourself and those around you. This is why I believe these seven shortcuts are the key to reclaiming not just your power but also your time, mental space, and direction. Remember the zero-point field I talked about in chapter 3? If you can create this space in your home and office, the heavy lifting shifts from being a burden that slows you down to enabling the quantum resonance techniques. It is the shortcut to your consistent well-being. You are the frequency leader here: the alpha—the tuning fork.

A space filled with coherent, continuous high vibes and a consciously designed energy field will dissolve the hard layer of frozen energy or blocks that have been stopping you and your clients from fulfilling their dreams. Your highest frequency can become your new normal. It can be your new "home frequency." Under your own steam, you can dissolve the hard shell of frozen or stuck consciousness that has been limiting you for years. I absolutely understand that you can dissipate the shell or the frozen tundra of stuck energy.

You don't need to be skyrocketed into dramatic, supernatural experiences far away, experiences that have been orchestrated by an external teacher or leader. I absolutely know that you can, under your own steam, dissolve the shell that separates you from a higher experience of Self and a high-quality life of your design and choosing. You don't need gurus or to be catapulted into supernatural experiences by dramatic events.

You have the potential to evolve in the present moment into a quantum, high-frequency being, right here in your physical body, with your family and in your own home frequency.

The Paranormal Dream Is
Your New Normal

What was once considered a paranormal dream is your new normal. You can become the new leader of your "tribe" of clients. By merely expanding your consciousness into this new reality of the 7 Quantum Hacks, you are capable of reaching your quantum potential in quantum speed and facilitating the transformation of your clients.

Living in the zero-point field of unlimited bliss and happiness is your new normal. You are able to attract the experiences and circumstances you desire and require to amplify your success and speed up your results on all levels. What used to be extraordinary is your new ordinary!

Step up now.

Everyone who chooses to live in the zero-point reality begins to resonate in a new octave, which revs up a gear, like a race car driver leading the track. You are in this quantum race together. Together, and as one, you can resonate into a higher-frequency realm where you all manifest faster with more consistent results. A zero-point field will demonstrate your place as a leader and transformer, where you can deliver shifts for your clients effortlessly and with flow, ease, and grace.

Let me share a story of a man who recently approached me.

This man (I'll call him Stuart) had spent all his savings on personal-development events, travel, and hotels in a short, one-year period. He was following one of the better-known personal-development gurus.

Stuart had spent all of his savings.

At the end of the year, he was left with some new knowledge, some great new friends, and the same fears he'd had before. I believe he had spent six figures. And yet, I became aware that Stuart's core subconscious issues were still percolating quite powerfully. By our first conversation, I realized that he had developed a deep fear that perhaps he would not be able to conquer these issues. His life circumstances—his job and his daily routine—had remained quite similar. But he was left with a longing to have more, to be freer, to conquer, to have his own business. He finally started to do the inner work when he ran out of money.

When Stuart was finally referred to us, he had reached a realization of the persistence of his fears, despite being entertained by the events, courses, and people he had encountered in the self-development world. He began to do his Voice Code Analysis daily, in the comfort of his own home, and found that the many emotions he had suppressed in his outward journey began to surface. His courage to confront these fears and unresolved emotions is what is carrying him to a higher level of coherence and peace. No longer seeking the external stimulation or joyride, he is now on the inner journey of his soul. He is finding his true heart-center again, but this time it is within him, so he does not have to seek the adrenaline rush of external events that used to stimulate him but not help him resolve the core issues of self-doubt, self-hatred, and persistent anxiety. This transformation occurring within the deep recesses of his soul will last him for a lifetime.

The Importance of Self-Love
for the Healer

As I said at the beginning of this chapter, many healer-coaches and people who follow the latest guru blame themselves for their failure to fully actualize the promise of the various teachings they learn about.

The most important quality for you, the healer-coach, is to learn total self-love in every cell of your body. Learn to imbibe this self-love as though it is the only thing that truly matters in this life. This is what is most rare. Then you can share this, model it, and retrieve this state at will.

Discharging, recharging, upwiring, and rewiring are all part of your cosmic awakening as a healer. I am giving you permission to find your sovereignty within yourself. You do not need to seek authority outside yourself. Know this, deeply.

PART III

Chapter 11

Only Fear Can Stop You Now

The Old (Downwired) You
Is Going to Resist

*Y*ou may come to this point and be wondering, "What if none of this is real? What if the 7 Quantum Hacks will not work for me? Is there enough scientific research backing this? What happens if my husband, wife, clients, children, friends do *not* resonate with the 7 Quantum Hacks? Does it matter?

"Is this all made-up BS?"

This is usually the point where your resistance to change rears its ugly head.

Let's choose to breathe and remain conscious here and now. The *old you* (the downwired you) is going to resist. This will likely take the form of extreme self-doubt. The ancient survival brain starts sending messages and destructive chemicals that could take control of you and keep you from moving forward.

We have unconsciously spent a lifetime creating something that many healers, personal-development experts, and coaches call the *comfort zone.*

Personally, I am sick to death of the term *comfort zone*, as it is overused in marketing and personal development, and as a result it has become a cliché, a turning point in the conversation through which someone gets you to buy something.

In conventional self-help and coaching, a comfort zone is the range of "what you have now" or "what you have created in your life now." It pretty much excludes everything you want but are too afraid (too uncomfortable) to pursue.

The comfort zone is surrounded by a series of messages generated by the primitive, two-thousand-year-old, downwired brain to stop you in your tracks and keep you from moving ahead and pursuing what your intuitive, higher self is leading you toward.

In simple, direct language, what will stop you is your fear. This fear is being generated by the primitive emotional brain. The primitive brain is only designed to keep you alive. It is not designed to awaken you to your full potential, to help you expand and grow.

You must learn to listen to these signals from the primitive brain as though they are junk emails—detect them and delete them before they get the best of you.

Just press delete, reboot, and reset.

Learn to ask yourself, "What is it that I really want to experience? Am I serving myself and my clients at the highest level? For my clients? And for myself?

"Am I on the high-speed elevator? Or am I plodding along in the basement of the subconscious?

"Am I truly getting the best results for my clients? Or can I improve these results by adding the missing modality?

"How can I improve the quality of life for myself as a healer? How can I prevent my own whole-life burnout from happening? Will a supercharged sanctuary really help me? How can I improve the quality of life for my clients? How can I accelerate the results in my healing work so that my clients are themselves on the fast track to the best life possible? If I were to design a Concorde turbojet experience—a platinum experience, the highest speed elevator in healing and transformation—what would I do? How can I serve at the highest level?"

Resist the temptation to downwire your brain and consciousness here.

Remember, rewiring and upwiring are the way to go. Downwiring returns you to the same rut you were in when you started.

Let's review the 7 Quantum Hacks. I'll keep it simple. We will revisit several of the key points made in the seven chapters in Part II, while bringing in new light and new ideas.

We have established that

- ✓ One modality alone in your life and healing business may not be creating the fastest, high-speed-elevator results that you desire for yourself and your clients. You may be missing an important component: the missing modality.

- ✓ You need to utilize an ongoing method of "discharging" the energy you are picking up. This will prevent whole-life burnout, which could result in stopping your healing work entirely, bottoming out and losing your livelihood and your investment.

- ✓ Self-healing and taking time for yourself is key to your ongoing well-being and thriving as a healer.

✓ You may be the one needing additional support to maintain your maximum mojo as a healer. This will help your clients both directly and indirectly.

✓ Some methods are complementary, rather than antithetical, to what you are doing. Integrating these into your existing practice could be accomplished quite effortlessly, with flow, ease, and grace, and no struggle.

✓ There are new paradigms and methods that may support your health and well-being and accelerate the results and impact of the modality you are working in.

That being said, we are also aware that many modalities and programs have been disappointing for you. You may even feel that these modalities have failed you or limited your expansion by not delivering the results needed to maintain your cutting edge and distinguish you from the pack.

This is particularly important in today's world, where there are so many healers. So many coaches. So many self-development experts. You need the **unfair advantage to stand out among the competition and become recognized for your gifts**. This is when your healing-coaching business will expand exponentially. You will then receive the accolades and satisfaction you deserve.

When you present, with ease and grace, the results people are seeking, your business will begin to thrive. Your clients will become your raving fans.

We have established that

✓ In whatever way you create your fortress of solitude, the process needs to be efficient and operate automatically, or you will forget or get too busy to do it.

✓ You need a precise way to interact with, decipher, and release your clients' subconscious codes—the ones running the show—but you don't have time to become the best psychologist on the planet.

✓ By deciphering your clients' subconscious codes, you will amplify the results of the modality you have spent years, and thousands of dollars, studying. Deciphering the subconscious of your clients will allow you to release the foundational traumas they have built their entire lives on. This will give you, and them, the freedom and clarity for optimal results in healing.

Now, what's stopping you? Your subconscious fears? The fear that if you change things, you will not remain the same?

You actually may have to transform how you are going about your life and business. Things will *feel* new and *be* new. You may go faster. You may become sought after. You may receive an unlimited flow of referrals. The primitive brain actually believes that you may die if you change, and signals you accordingly.

So, I ask you again: **Are you ready to transform?**

I have learned one thing through my many years of being human. Most people fear and resist change of all kinds. Even change they have asked for, repeatedly visualized, gone to Egypt to create, prayed for, intended, attracted, divined.

The successful ones have learned to feel the fear and do it **anyway!**

In this chapter, I will give you fair warning of what is going to happen when you set this book down, so you can be prepared—and so you can keep moving forward into ever more of the experience you really want.

I know you put your heart and soul into your healing business. You are amazing at what you do. You likely have earned endless certifications after countless hours of dedicated work, and you truly have a desire to help people and serve. Many of you wish to help thousands of people during your lifetime.

In this book, I have unveiled the secret process that will allow you to shine and be even more brilliant in your work, without adding a huge weight to your workload. Instead, the workload (or the weight of it) will become lighter as you practice with these 7 Quantum Hacks.

The 7 Quantum Hacks Constitute a Formula to Prevent Burnout!

I have shared the 7 Quantum Hacks that will skyrocket your results and keep you in your zone of genius so that you can co-create with spirit and help thousands of people to awaken, to heal, and to improve the quality of their lives. This formula will help you get even better results and ensure that you will spend your lifetime thriving while you transform those who are drawn to you.

The secret miracle ingredient I have revealed involves getting your clients to vibrate at higher levels. This works to support and solidify the work you are already trained in. The great news for you is that it is simple and precise and will work effortlessly.

One of the saddest aspects of those in the healing business is that they do not fully understand the true nature of discharging the energy they absorb from working with their clients. They believe they can keep doing their work without any consequence. I myself learned many years ago from a modern-day Indian avatar that this is why many healers in the West become ill after a few years of practice.

Take a moment. Do you seriously discharge the energy that may be transferred to you during your work? Are you always at your best when you see your clients?

In the interior regions of your brain, you are taking in four million bits of information every second. It comes in through your optical system, every nerve, your auditory system, your olfactory system, your sense of taste—everything. Every nerve in your entire body system communicates with the reticular activating system, which then filters down all of the four million bits into about two thousand bits. This is a tiny fraction of the information actually available to you. We are never receiving the whole picture of what is actually available to us.

> *People like us, who believe in physics, know that the distinction between past, present, and future is only a stubbornly persistent illusion.*
>
> Albert Einstein,
> quoted in *Disturbing the Universe*
> by Freeman Dyson

Many will try to stop you from pursuing your dream of raising your frequency and the frequency of your clients and tribe, and thereby living your ideal life. I want to warn you at this point that if you listen to others' opinions, you could be led astray.

If you follow this formula, you will save money on endless courses and make more money from clients, due to your high-level focus, creativity, and bliss, which make you effortlessly attractive to your tribe.

You will become the master of your fate and destiny, instead of giving your power away to others who are more than willing to steal it away from you.

Some of the obstacles that could come up are

✓ You could be plagued with so much self-doubt that you feel you cannot possibly do this.

✓ You may start to feel waves of self-doubt, hatred, or insecurity, and you might project this and doubt the worth of this work.

✓ You could lose self-confidence by not listening to your inner intuition and voice.

✓ You may feel that you cannot afford this (both time-wise and financially). Truly, you cannot afford not to do this.

In this work I have presented a repeatable, precise, simple, sound method of transformation. You can integrate these 7 Quantum Hacks effortlessly to support you and your existing practice.

Obstacle 1:
"I Don't Have the Time"

So, what are the obstacles to your stepping up to experiment with the 7 Quantum Hacks? I can almost sense the response of obstacle one: "Well, this sounds great, but I simply don't have the time or energy."

Precisely my point. You don't have the energy! You have reached the burnout zone.

Something is missing if you as a healer-coach find yourself without time or energy.

You need to be the one *with* the energy, the insight, the wisdom. You need to hold the space. My hacks offer an alternative, to gather more positive energy and discharge lower-vibrational energy automatically and effortlessly.

Obstacle 2: Complexity

What happens if this is too complicated to learn and know? You say, "I've spent years acquiring an in-depth knowledge of my primary modality. What happens if this new modality takes as much time?"

Thankfully, it won't. My point precisely, again. This modality can be mastered in one hour of your time. You plug it into a power outlet. You can also choose to use the Voice Code Analysis process for yourself and your clients. This will take about forty-five minutes in training. It's straightforward: take a voice sample, generate a soundtrack, play it for your client, and voila! It's done.

While that may sound simple, these personalized, unique soundtracks are the hack that will penetrate your subconscious and the stubborn subconscious of each of your beautiful clients. You don't have to go in depth—the technology will do it for you. It is as precise as anything on planet earth—more so. We give you the tool you need, and you can use it without having to do years of study, analysis, and training. It is designed to be complementary to everything you have practiced to date. A hack into your subconscious. It's like being handed all the test answers just before you turn in your exam paper—only far more ethical.

We know that we are all in resonance with the collective consciousness, and this Voice Code Analysis is precisely what we need to shift. Once the shift transforms us to a higher vibration, our manifestation and quantum potential manifest effortlessly.

Obstacle 3:
Your Self-Doubt and Lack Paradigm

The degree to which you doubt your intuition, insight, and knowledge is the degree to which you experience lack. Those who prosper have given up self-doubt for the higher frequency of self-love and are actualizing their unlimited quantum potential. With the information I provide in this book, you will have what you need, once you decide this is a path that will make your life and practice easier and will magnify your results as a healer-coach. Your belief will manifest whatever funds you need.

Obstacle 4:
Frozen in Fear and Self-Doubt

Here's the deal: your limiting beliefs exist on a subconscious level. That's the mind trap. That's also the healer-coach trap and why many never fulfill their potential. These subconscious beliefs are held at the level of frequency and ultimately manifest on the physical level. I see them as frozen blocks of energy that prevent flow.

My lifetime of observation has shown me that the subconscious is always manifesting in front of us, but most seem to live in a continual state of denial and projection, denying what is in front of their eyes as a manifestation, and pushing it away.

A question I am frequently asked by our prospective clients is "Why is the law of attraction not working for me even though I have been practicing for fifteen years?" The answer is always simple: you are functioning on the surface, while your subconscious continues to run the show. The problem is that most seek the answers outside themselves, in the most obvious places.

The answer is very clear to me. The universe is delivering what it is designed for: to act as a mirror of our subconscious. The frequency you are vibrating, the resonance and coherence you feel, they are replayed back to you. Your subconscious, limiting beliefs vibrate out and draw certain experiences to you.

Obstacle 5:
External Skepticism

Your significant other doubts you. The enlightened way to resolve this is to realize that at some fundamental level, your significant other is a projection of you. We have found that when your true self and intuition take the lead, your significant other will thank you in the end, as they will benefit from your transformation and transform themselves, living in the coherence of zero-point energy. We have had significant others (those who are resistant at first) get promotions, stop drinking alcohol, and stop arguing incessantly about trivial matters. My advice is always to follow your intuition, take the leap of faith, and trust yourself in matters of your own evolution. Everyone around you will benefit from this quantum leap of faith!

CHAPTER 12

My Wish for You

Why I Wrote This Book at This Time

I wrote this book as a way for you and me to connect. I trusted that synchronicity would align when you needed this most. Robert and I have been developing this therapeutic quantum sound modality for over forty years, but it's only now that we feel the call to be more public in how we reach those who will enact positive life changes forever. It might sound too woo-woo for you, but when you analyze why you're on this journey with us, I believe you too will identify the alignment.

Let me state the big reveal—we offer all 7 Quantum Hacks together in the Quantum Sound Miracle iQube package. It includes the Miracle itself, all the soundtracks I've mentioned, the Voice Code Analysis software, and the structured water. Robert and I are very excited to extend the entire package to you at this time. Even as global technological advancements have resulted in dirtying the earth's energy, we have dedicated our lives to improving the quality of people's lives.

You may feel on the surface that this is a synchronicity. In reality, the work has appeared because you have been asking—seeking a modality that would effortlessly change things, that would deal with the subconscious of your clients' sabotage, and that would simplify your life for the better and cut through the BS. Also, you've been seeking a modality that might uplift you without your having to feed it, so that you could remain in your own zone of genius and feel awesome while you serve others.

Our modality is not as well known at this time as Reiki, feng shui, or yoga—but I believe it is the healer-coach add-on you need for your business. Do you remember the first time you heard of feng shui? Or Bikram yoga? Or float tanks? Yet soon they became part of our vernacular and no longer a hippies-only health concept.

This, we know, is what will happen with Quantum Sound Therapy, because the results speak for themselves. When you bring in frequency-clearing practices and feel the increased vibrations and the release of stagnant mind trauma, you will want that for your friends and family too.

For now, before your home and office is vibrating at the levels you have been subconsciously striving for, you have intuitively joined me on this journey and begun to appreciate and comprehend the value of adding this breakthrough modality to your life and your business. Whether you commit now or experiment with the exercises and bonus tracks included in this book, at least sound therapy is on your radar as a healer-coach business owner.

You're committed to helping others, your community, and the planet, but as you have a healer-coach business, it is really all about you. What you can give and impart to the clients seeking your help does not happen miraculously. You have to be aligned, attuned, and balanced. Consider the Quantum

Sound Miracle iQube as your tuning fork—the shortcut that will create the desired energy. The gift that will keep on giving energy back to you, no matter how depleted you may feel at times. Your daily growth and commitment to yourself is why your client base has been growing. When you elevate your evolution and expand your healing footprint, your visibility soars. It is still just about you, and this change to your community is reliant on you.

The stress you have felt managing and growing your successful healing business is also intuitively felt by your clients. As many of the popular healing and coaching modalities on the planet have become instantly available through a three-second Google search, so has the competition to obtain excellent results and raving fans that are drawn to you. Your elevated vibration is what will draw your ideal clients to you. Broadcasting your message through your high-frequency vibration and coherence is what you will require in the years to come to maintain and expand your healer-coach business. If you are thrashing around like a small boat on a turbulent ocean, your ideal clients will be repelled, regardless of the excellence of your work or modality. You need the unfair advantage that will maintain your vibrations consistently, to help others raise their vibrations.

Will you be able to uplift your clients' frequencies consistently with this modality so that they will commit to a continued practice with you? And refer their friends and loved ones to you? Yes—if you can uplift them to a level beyond their imagination. When you do this, they become your raving fans and loyal members of your tribe. They effectively end up doing the lion's share of your marketing for you, too.

When you use our products, you enhance your clients' receptivity while reducing their resistance. They optimize their personal ability to absorb your healer-coach practices. They finally dissipate their subconscious blocks. Without any new training required of you. It's a miraculous hack; hence why one of our products is called the Miracle. We have been striving to design and implement technology that effortlessly aligns with whatever healing modality you practice. Our algorithms do the heavy lifting, which can only mean more time for you.

When you have "me time," you are not drained by business practices. You can remain passionate and committed to your life's work and without further strain. No doubt you pursued this career path as a calling, not a money-making machine. You wanted to help, to serve, to add some love to your clients' lives. To improve the quality of their lives, relationships, and well-being through their work with you.

How I Want You to Feel Now

My goal for this book is not just to get my products into your hands—though of course I'll be happy if you join me in my mission and purpose. I want you to know that there is a way to get out of the healing trap and free yourself from the merry-go-round and the roller coaster.

Forget running a schedule, accounting, sales, marketing, and juggling the finances for your business. It's a trap: you spend more time swimming in toffee to keep your business afloat and less time maintaining your healer-coach flow and in turn supporting people to transform. This then leads to an increase in stress, inadequacy, doubt, and worse. Then you need more courses or retreats to maintain your balance and uplift your soul to its rightful vibration. It's a trap with the potential for physical and energetic bankruptcy. But you're no hamster. It's time to escape the wheel and run for your freedom.

"Oh, wow, Helena," you might say. "You sound like you're speaking from experience."

I am. I got burned out, with chronic fatigue and a ten-year-old I barely had the energy to care for. On paper I looked successful, with a four-month waiting list and CNBC speaking engagements, but it wasn't delivered from a place of peace, and therefore I was doomed for the anxiety to catch up with me.

My modalities—the ones I include in this book—saved my life. Due to this, it became my mission to serve and uplift the healer-coach community. Consider this book my way to reach out my hand as the quicksand pulls you down further into density and resistance.

There will always be resistance; perhaps you're feeling it as you read this. You've reached chapter 12 and still don't trust your reason for continuing to invest your time in my message. You've met the healer's paradox before, though, in your practice, when someone asks for help and then is unable to receive what you offer. This is the land of broken dreams for you, because although you have done your very best to uplift them, they resist you and your efforts. This also creates an invisible energy drain that bankrupts you over time.

I want the light to go on for you: there is something out there that is "straight outta quantum" to heal the healers—and help the servers live lives of quality, fulfillment, and purpose.

A Review of What We've Covered

Let's take another look at the 7 Quantum Hacks.

Hack 1: Your Peaceful Space

Hack 1 is the creation of your peaceful space through quantum clearing. I describe the principles of designing the subtle energy of your space to act as a clearing and discharging vortex, something that will cleanse and uplift you. I explain why such a supportive space is vital to you as a healer-coach.

The significance of understanding the field you are living in and how to redesign it to support, uplift, and discharge the energies you may have attracted during the day is essential. We also covered the concept of entrainment with the positive, and how to create a field using Quantum Sound technology that automatically relaxes, releases, entrains, and discharges you in your clinic and/or home.

Hack 2: Voice Code Analysis

Hack 2 utilizes quantum attunement through the little-known modality of Voice Code Analysis to detect and release your clients' subconscious blocks, so they become more receptive to your modality and receive your work without resistance.

For a free "Find Your Frequency" consult with me, go to calendly.com/quantumsoundtherapy.

Hack 3: Unleashing Your Genius

Through quantum activation, Hack 3 enhances neuroplasticity by unleashing the power of the left frontal lobe. I explain how activating the left frontal lobe will effortlessly enhance your results. By hacking your subconscious, you hack your future timeline. Your subconscious is an unseen force that you must harness and empower.

Hack 4: Awakening the Third Eye

Quantum awakening of our intuition by decalcifying and awakening the third eye is Hack 4. Through enhanced results, we engage the law of intent. All great masters, teachers, and coaches have an open and active pineal gland and third eye. Do you want to join them?

Hack 5: Repatterning through Delta Deep Sleep

Hack 5 explains the quantum healing and repatterning that occurs through delta sleep. It is possible that your best inner work is done while sleeping. A deep delta entrainment zone provides us with refreshing sleep and lucid dreaming.

Hack 6: High-Vibe Structured Water

Hack 6 employs quantum imprinting through the imbibing of high-vibe structured water, structured to be geometrically coherent with the cells of the body.

Hack 7: Take Back Your Power

Through quantum awareness, Hack 7 enables you to connect directly to your own power and your own healing field in your home and office. This makes the healing trap—the endless self-development trap—totally unnecessary. My wish is that you stop once and for all, and get off the merry-go-round of giving too much and receiving too little.

My wish for you is also that you find this missing modality that supports you to take back your intuitive power as a healer-coach and stop giving total power and surrender to modalities that are external to your own inner voice. My wish for you is that you thrive on all levels in your business as a healer-coach.

Conclusion

In summary, my truest wish for you is that you become an *awakened healer-coach!* The world needs awakened healers and healer-coaches. They are givers with a passion, a purpose, and a mission.

I wish that you may live an unencumbered life of brilliance, freedom, and clarity, where you will see deeply into your own issues and the issues being reflected by your clients.

I wish that you may get off the endless merry-go-round of the healing trap. I would love you to be someone with a mission to serve and help others rise with you.

My wish for you is that you thrive and shine in your brilliance!

References

Arntz, William, Betsy Chasse, Mark Vicente. *What the Bleep Do We Know!?*

Asprey, Dave. *Game Changers.*

Braden, Gregg. *Awakening to Zero Point: The Collective Initiation.*

Dispenza, Joe. *Breaking the Habit of Being Yourself.*

———. Evolve Your Brain.

Emoto, Masaru. *The True Power of Water: Healing and Discovering Ourselves.*

Gardner, Kay. *Sounding the Inner Landscape: Music as Medicine.*

Goswami, Amit. The Quantum Doctor: A Quantum Physicist Explains the Healing Power of Integral Medicine.

Huffington, Arianna. *The Sleep Revolution: Transforming Your Life, One Night at a Time.*

Jhon, Mu Shik. *The Water Puzzle and the Hexagonal Key.*

About the Author

Helena Reilly, MA, is the co-creator and co-founder of Quantum Sound Therapy. Together with her partner, Robert Lloy, she invented the Quantum Sound Miracle iQube, a sound and scalar vortex technology that transforms subconscious patterns. Helena is a pioneer and expert in the use of sound frequencies and scalar vortex technology to effect profound transformation.

In 2015, Who's Who of Distinguished Alumni awarded Helena for her breakthrough work co-founding Quantum Sound Therapy, a therapeutic modality that is capable of bold, efficient, and lasting transformation. Helena has discussed this new paradigm work as a guest on CNBC and worldwide radio shows and telesummits. She authored her first book, *Sound Energetics*, to reveal her private practice work in New York City. From birth, Helena has been a highly sensitive person, a healer who is gifted with claircognizance, clairsentience, and clairaudience.

After completing her graduate work in the therapeutic treatment of individuals, families, and groups at the University of Chicago, Helena searched the world for impactful modalities. Serving as a psychotherapist in the ashrams of some of the leading contemporary Indian spiritual masters, she learned that even in the presence of an enlightened master, many are unable to resolve their root pain patterns and remain stuck. In India, she discovered the ancient secret that entrainment with sound frequencies facilitates shifts in brain wave states that alleviate depression and PTSD.

As a master intuitive, Helena resolved to dedicate her life to finding a bold, breakthrough, practical solution to help people get unstuck and to free them from the bondage of these patterns. Quantum Sound Therapy is the answer to that search.

In 2002, Helena left her private practice in New York to join her twin flame, co-founder, and the creator of Scalar Wave technology, Robert Lloy. Since then, they have applied their wisdom and knowledge to co-create the Miracle iQube and the Tesla iQube, Miracle Structured Water, and award-winning Voice Analysis software.

The award-winning Voice Analysis software developed by Robert Lloy analyses over one-and-a-half billion bits of information to create a unique and personalized twenty-seven-minute holographic soundtrack that boldly clears deep redundant patterns from a person's energy field. Together, they have also developed software based on voice assessment to find and harmonize a client's unique personal frequency, now available through quantumsoundtherapy.com/cloud-sound-therapy.

These many elements of the Quantum Sound Therapy system are designed to raise the resonance of your environment and your energy field on a 24-7 plug-and-play basis.

Thank You

Thank you for reading my book.

I'd like to offer you a free gift as a way to say thank you, by offering you a free webinar: "7 Quantum Hacks to Transform Your Healing Business" at quantumsoundtherapy.com/wp-content/uploads/2019/07/Zoom-Session-May-16-2019-7-Quantum-Hacks-Audio-Only.mp3.

If you'd like to chat further, I'd love to hear from you. Feel free to reach out to me at helena@quantumsoundtherapy.com. Just schedule here: calendly.com/quantumsoundtherapy! I look forward to hearing from you.

Website: quantumsoundtherapy.com

Also visit us on social media:

Facebook: quantumsoundtherapy
Instagram: @quantumsoundtherapy

www.quantumsoundtherapy.com

50% off Cloud Sound Therapy (Voice Code Analysis Online) 1 Session Available on Apple & Windows 10 Platforms Coupon Code "7 Quantum Hacks"